I Lost My Baby,

My Pickup,

and My Guitar

on the

Information Highway

I Lost My Baby, My Pickup, and My Guitar

on the

INFORMATION HIGHWAY

A Humorous Trip Down the Highways, Byways, and Backroads of Information Technology

Judy Heim

No Starch Press
Daly City, California

Publisher: William Pollock

Cover & Interior Design: Cloyce Wall

Compositor: Steven Bolinger

Copyeditors: William Rodarmor, Kathryn Hashimoto

Cartoon Illustrations: Brian McMurdo, Ventana Studio, Valley Center, California. All cartoons copyright Ventana Studios.

Printed in the United States of America
1 2 3 4 5 6 7 8 9 10—99 98 97 96 95

Printed on acid-free recycled paper.

Trademarks
Trademarked names are used throughout this book. Rather than use a trademark symbol with every occurrence of a trademarked name, we are using the names only in an editorial fashion and to the benefit of the trademark owner, with no intention of infringement of the trademark.

Library of Congress Cataloging-in-Publication Data
Heim, Judy.
    I lost my baby, my pickup, and my guitar on the information highway: a humorous trip down the highways, byways, and back-roads of information technology / Judy Heim.
        p. cm.
    ISBN 1-886411-00-X
    1. Information technology—Humor. I. Title.
T58.5.H45   1995
004'.0207—dc20   94-46713

Distributed to the book trade in the United States and Canada by Publishers Group West, P.O. Box 8843, Emeryville, California 94662, 800-788-3123.

For information on translations or book distributors outside the United States, please write to:

No Starch Press
1903 Jameston Lane, Daly City, CA 94014-3466
415-334-7200

Dedication

To the memory of my father, Jordan Beechie Getts, a man who bought all his power tools at Sears, relished his *Popular Sciences*, drove only Buicks, could rewire toasters and lamps with the best of them, believed that anything that was battery-powered had to be good, and never went anywhere without a screwdriver. The only disappointment he ever gave me was that he was not around long enough to see what a darned invention the personal computer was. God bless him.

Contents

Acknowledgments

This book would be nothing but a rumpled manuscript with coffee-stains on it if not for the creativity and hard work of one of the most gifted bands of editors and artists I've ever worked with. First, there was Robert Luhn, the book's unofficial godfather. Robert is the kind of guy who simply has to say, "Make it zany!" and suddenly the creative mud flows. William Rodarmor has always been kind enough to support my goofball writing schemes, but this time he went the distance and his skillful editing pulled the book out of its disorder into the realm of elegant prose. Steve Bass's wit and encouragement saved the day on more than one occasion.

Brian McMurdo of Ventana Studio lent his gentle humor to the pages with cartoons that delight me each time I flip a page. The brilliant Cloyce Wall astonished us with a witty cover design that helped to reassure us that we had left behind the world of run-of-the-mill computer books for good. He is also to thank for the book's interior design. Steven Bolinger scrambled to fit all the pieces of the book's puzzle together as the last hours ticked by.

Vicki Friedberg worked over the final pages tirelessly with a pencil to make sure they were good enough for other people to read. Kathy Hashimoto also labored with red pen to ensure that past participles were truly past.

Finally, Bill Pollock proved himself the best publisher a writer could have, showing enthusiasm, intelligence, and spunk at every turn—not to mention a willingness to entertain ideas that ordinary publishers would scoff at.

A hearty thank you to all.

And, oh yes, a special thank you to my husband, John, for always being ready with beer, sympathy, or a TV dinner, depending on what was needed to weather the rigors of a writer's life.

I Lost My Baby,

My Pickup,

and My Guitar

on the

Information Highway

Prologue

What Is the Information Highway?

L ast winter, a rumor started on some computer bulletin board that I had met my husband on the info-highway. More specifically, we had met, according to this rumor, in a raunchy public message conference called "Bull Roar and More." (A computer bulletin board is like a mini-computer information service. BBS's are run by computer hobbyists, often in their basements. People from all over the country are free to call the BBS with their computers and leave messages to others. BBS's are the electronic equivalent of the corner tavern, where no one is ever thrown out, most people ought to be, and some people are rumored to have passed two to three decades of their lives.)

I was soon deluged with phone calls from every newspaper reporter in the country writing a "Valentine's Day on the Information Highway" story. (They were all seeking lovers who had trysted via modem.)

The clincher came when a public television station called. They were filming a documentary on the Information Highway and wanted to include me. I was extremely flattered. However, when they found out that my husband and I hadn't actually met on a BBS (we met through a computer dating service), they were no longer interested in interviewing me.

Has that painful experience caused me to become bitter about the Information Highway? Maybe. I have always wanted to be in a PBS documentary, and the fact that I was passed over because I was never a modem-bride shall be a lifelong disappointment. But before I let the documentary maker hang up, I insisted on telling him exactly what the Information Highway is, all the way to its signaling bandwidth specifications. Similarly, I am going to tell you exactly what it is, and I don't want to hear any guff about it.

What Is the Info-Highway? A Primer   If you watch a lot of TV, you probably think the Information Highway is owned by long-distance phone companies. That's what they want you to believe.

If you read the newspaper business section, you probably think the Information Highway is owned by some cable TV company. That's what *they* want you to believe.

In reality, "the Information Highway" is nothing more than a phrase that Vice-President Al Gore muttered when it came to light that the White House didn't even have a working fax machine. No one could have predicted the mud slide of national hyperbole that would follow, not to mention all the truly insipid multimillion dollar ad campaigns featuring little girls standing in big fields babbling nonsense.

The backbone of the Information Highway is something called Internet (that's right, you hear about the Internet almost daily). Internet was originally a computer network linking military contractors, universities, and the Defense Department. Just like everything else that was ever specifically designed for advancing the aims of the Pentagon, it didn't take long for the rest of the world to find out how keen it was and demand access to it. Soon, everyone in the world was linked into Internet. Now, even communist China is a part of it. Most basement BBS's are, too.

By using Internet, you can send electronic mail to almost anyone in the world, from envoys at United Nations' offices in Uzbekistan to computer bulletin board users in the Philippines. You can send computer files to universities in Saudi Arabia and spreadsheets to clients at Fortune 500 corporations and swap E-mail with pals on commercial computer services like Prodigy and America Online. You can also travel Internet to tap into computers at universities and government agencies and access lots of extremely useful databases like the one at Dartmouth which holds over six hundred years' worth of line-by-line commentary on Dante's *Divine Comedy*.

If you're thinking, "Wait a minute! I bet I can use Internet to become a reviled international spy!" you're absolutely right. And if you're thinking, "Hold on! I bet I could waste a lot of time on Internet, fooling around playing computer games while my boss thinks I'm using Internet to research Israeli electro-optics and getting all sorts of work done," you're right too. Internet, properly used, can be the ultimate time sink. Why do you think the government has put so much money into it? Many great minds have been known to log on and never rematerialize.

It's no surprise then that ever since Al Gore's testimonial, Internet has grown into a national repository of technologically subliterate goof-offs, sociopaths, crazies, and aspiring international fiends (a possible reason why Rush Limbaugh refuses to read any E-mail that comes to him with an Internet address). Even the White House is now on Internet (whitehouse@gov).

The Telephone Company Tie-In   Aside from Internet and all the computers connected to it, there is another important facet to the Information Highway. That's the futuristic phone service part. Imagine that you took all the marketing and public relations minds from all the phone companies in the world. You gave everyone a writing tablet; you sent them off to one of those $15K per person corporate retreats where they can play golf all day, attend an occasional motivation seminar, and jot down their innermost thoughts. One of the assignments you give them is, "Write down all the things that someone might be able to do with a phone someday and which you think are really cool." That is what telephone aspect of the Information Highway is. Its formulation is not far from that scenario.

The basic idea is that the phone companies are going to pull out all the copper phone cable that's running to your house and replace it with a fiber optic cable. That fiber optic cable will be capable of transmitting to you not just one or two phone calls at a time, but movies, computer data, and phone calls all at once. The problem is that the whole thing's much more complicated than just digging up your lawn and planting a translucent filament that looks like it was pulled from a bong-bong lamp at Spencer Gifts.

The phone companies will have to replace their phone switches too. In many cases they'll have to replace their phone switches with ones that work. That in itself is going to prove a major obstacle to the phone network of the future. Right now many phone companies are replacing their switches with ones that don't work with high-speed faxes. Some, I have heard, are replacing their switches with ones that don't work with computer modems. Some are even replacing their switches with ones that won't work with voices. That is not a good sign for the Information Highway. My personal feeling is that if you can't phone out for pizza without the connection sounding like you're lost in a sandstorm in the Gobi desert, how can any cable company expect to someday transmit *Rambo*, complete and uninterrupted over your phone wire?

I remember the first time I heard about this plan I was skeptical. It was over a decade ago, and I was living with my mother at the time. I was a budding journalist so I was living in her basement. One morning she woke me up at 6:30. "It's the vice-president of AT&T," she screamed. She shook my shoulder vigorously. "I knew I shouldn't have let you install that phone in the basement. I just knew it!" she gasped, as we ran down the basement steps in our bathrobes and bouncing foam curlers. "You didn't pay the phone bill on time and now the vice-president of AT&T is calling to repossess our house!"

When I picked up the phone it was indeed a vice-president from AT&T. He wanted to tell me about their plans for a futuristic phone system. As I scribbled down the initials I asked, "But you're going to have to replace like, phone wires and stuff?" (I was pleased to note that the vice-president of AT&T was big enough not to snicker when I used the phrase "like, phone wires and stuff." But then, he was probably used to talking to the press.) "There will need to be some modifications at the local switching centers," he conceded. Right then, as I looked up at the wilted phone wire curling its way down the basement wall, sprouting from a gaping hole blasted haphazardly through the cinder block in the house's foundation, I knew that the whole concept was doomed.

At the time, the futuristic phone system was just a telephone company pipe dream. But since then, cable and movie companies have decided they want to be part of the action too, and they too have been busy thinking up things that they can transmit to your house over phone lines and charge lots of money for. The 900-number "psychic friends" chat lines are apparently only the beginning. In the future, you'll be able dial up old sitcoms and order cubic zirconium jewelry and other things you once needed a cable company installer to give you the ability to do. Personally, I think life is complicated enough just having a phone that jangles day and night with calls from people you don't want to talk to. But then, it was only a couple years ago that I conceded that Touch-Tone dialing was the wave of the future and signed up to have the service on my phone line.

To Sum Up   So that, my friend, is what the Information Highway is. It is a military-inspired computer network that got out of control. It is a futuristic phone system that will deliver futuristic promises, like old sitcoms and infomercials over your phone line, at prices you probably will not be able to afford. And it is million-dollar marketing.

The thing I find most amazing about the emerging infobahn is that people actually think they can get things done on it. Many even think that being on it will advance their careers by allowing them to network with powerful, well-connected professionals like themselves. In actuality, the only reason most people are on the info-highway is because there's nothing on TV, plain and simple. If you don't believe me, remember this: the busiest public electronic message string in the entire world is devoted to *Star Trek*—an almost thirty-year-old TV show in which the bad guy aliens look like dissipated Shakespearean actors!

This book is about the info-highway, and in keeping with the spirit of the info-highway engineering specifications, it has no plan or order whatsoever. It is just a collection of idle musings, a few tall tales, some bawdy jokes, and offhand quips inspired by life with a computer modem—the sorts of things cowboys might relate between tobacco chews, while sitting around a fire to entertain each other after a long day.

The first computer bulletin board I ever logged on to was run by a military contractor in Maryland. The first E-mail message I ever received consisted of a scatological, sexist quip so uninspired its author could not have been anything other than a 15-year-old boy (though he was probably in his 30s). I don't remember what I typed in response, only that it was one line. Within hours I received a chorus of E-mail "bravos!" from male computer hackers, and the cad lost any hope of future access to the board. I, on the other hand, was warmly welcomed into a world that I had feared I would never be admitted to.

That was years ago. That call to a BBS led to a career I never would have expected, and a score of friends and adventures I'm generally unable to recount anyplace other than in "cyberspace" for fear of being considered an outright lunatic. After that call to the military contractor bulletin board, I never received another rude E-mail message. Not one in a decade of calling bulletin boards and computer online services and mouthing off about everything from politics to home cooking to feminism.

That doesn't mean that cyberspace is a particularly polite world. To the contrary, it's like any Wild West frontier. It's lawless, anarchic, full of bad characters, and you never know when a wanted scoundrel lurks beneath a white hat. Just like in any frontier town, civility often erupts in shootouts, and rudeness is frequently justified with cries of "Free speech!" But it is a highly egalitarian society nonetheless, accessible to anyone with a computer keyboard and a phone line. Its members are generally warm and receptive to anyone with something interesting to say. For those simple reasons, the Information Highway is a wonderful place for anyone to be—whether woman, man, or articulate primate. Although admittedly most people on it would qualify for the latter category.

Welcome aboard.

How to Figure Out How Much
E-mail You Will Get

Your first year on the Information Highway will be an exciting one. You'll probably get lots of E-mail. But how much E-mail will you get? Here is an easy calculation you can perform to figure out just how much.

Start by counting the number of cubic feet of file space in your office. Multiply it by the estimated articles of junk mail you receive annually. Square this by the number of digits in your modem's brand name (as in HSZ-Express 14200).

Office Cubic Feet × Per Annum Junk Mail Influx (X^2 Real Integers in Modem's Name$)^2$ + Total Business Cards in Rolodex Sum Variance

Add the number of business cards in your Rolodex. Move the decimal point to the right by as many places as pairs of running shoes you own. Square that by the number of chips you think are in your computer.

(Number of Pairs of Running Shoes × 10) (X^2 Theoretical Guestimate of Chips in Your PC$)^2$

Add the number of appliances in your house. Multiply it by the number of phone lines coming into your office. Multiply this by the number of phone lines going into your co-workers' offices. Cube this by the number of cable TV channels you have ever watched in your lifetime.

Household Appliance Count Probability Density Factor × Phone Line Traffic × Phone Line Traffic > Co-workers' Standard Deviation (X^2 Total Number of Cable TV Channels You Have Watched)

Now plot this number as a vector you know, the sort of line that shoots off the side of the graph in the upper corner, like so

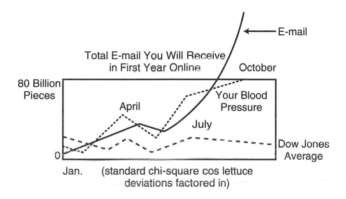

Now, wasn't that simple? Welcome to the Information Age!

Where to Find the Most Bizarre
Public E-mail Discussions

Information Highway Tip #2087

I n the normal, workaday world, flagrant eccentricity
sometimes proves a liability—the purple spiked hair behind the bank counter, the caftan with the sun and the moon
worn to lunch with the Rotarians. But in cyberspace, on the
many freewheeling computer information services dotting
the Information Highway, the madcap is celebrated, vener-
ated, and catered to.

You may find that the public message conference for
UFO watchers is listed on the same menu
as the one for the Young Republicans.
You may spot the "Masonic
Metaphysics" forum listed
on your computer screen
right beside that for
"Collectors of China
Dolls." Or you may
find that the mes-
sages in the "Alter-
native Lifestyles"
public computer
forum are automatically carbon-copied into the "Yeast
Breads Made by Hand" forum, so that participants of both
forums can participate in the conversations simultaneously.
In cyberspace, anything is possible.

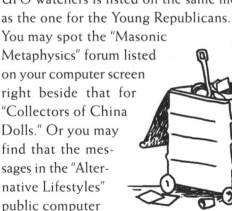

What is a computer message forum? It's the computer age equivalent of a truck stop coffee shop. People wander in and out at all times of the day and night; they type messages to each other—even to strangers. They leave eloquent replies. They rap, argue, and pontificate on whatever subject moves them.

The most bizarre message forum in cyberspace is unquestionably "talk.bizarre" (pronounced "talk-dot-bizarre"). It can be found in the Usenet messages on Internet. There the greatest minds from academia join with those from government and the private sector to pontificate on rock 'n' roll, the pitfalls of cloning one's spouse, a sinister fictitious corporation referred to as "X-Industries," and other, well, bizarrities. About every tenth message ends with the admonition "Getalife!"

Commercial information services are not without their own talk-dot-bizarres. The New Age forum on CompuServe offers special message areas for topics like "Esoteric Societies," "Tarot & Oracles," and "UFOlogy/Contacts." On a recent visit, participants were organizing a confab of sorts in which, on a selected evening at a specified time, everyone would sit down and simultaneously try to contact UFOs by mental telepathy. There were a lot of volunteers.

The Left Coast Naturists Online message area on General Electric's GEnie offers nudists their daily dose of nudist talk in forums with names like "Nude in the News." GEnie's thousands of hobby conferences cater to many unlikely passions, including "Tattoo Appreciation and Collecting," graveyard and tombstone watching, grocery coupon clipping (one regular message string in this forum is titled "Dumpster Diving"), and collecting fast food memorabilia.

It is somehow reassuring to know that some of the most heavily trafficked conferences on GEnie, Prodigy, and CompuServe are the ones devoted to quilting. The embroidery message areas are also hot. On the other hand, it is somewhat disquieting to note that the most heavily trafficked E-mail conference worldwide is the *Star Trek* news group on Internet. Readers may write an awesome thousand or more messages in it in a single weekend after an episode of an especially thought-provoking *Star Trek* spin-off show airs.

One of the most peculiar message threads I have ever stumbled across was in Internet's football conference. It centered around an argument over whether Canada should be considered an "overseas nation." Had this discussion taken place in a corner bar, the participants would have been lampooned as a bunch of dumb jocks. Not in cyberspace. The argument ended with participants agreeing that technically, yes, Canada could be considered "overseas," not because of Lake Erie, but because Canada is a different country from the United States. At least they got that part right.

Come to think of it, cyberspace is a lot like the corner bar.

Do Not Computer-Fax Marriage Proposals to People Unless You Are Sure How to Use Your Fax Software

Information Highway Tip #2914

T his is a fax that recently reached the customer service department of a major corporation:

Aloha,

To update you with what's going on, I talked with the priest, and he said that all he would need is a letter from your priest in Atlanta showing that you have completed the courses to prepare you for marriage. He would need three to four months' notice. The only thing that Hawaii requires is for you to get a rubella test. I called the State Health Dept, and they will send you a package. If you don't get this package soon, let me know.

The Audi is undergoing a major wax job with sandpaper.

The pictures are of George.

Have a great new year. I love you.

Lloyd

Customer service decided the problem, if any, wouldn't be covered by warranty. They filed the fax under "R" for rubella, and waited.

The PC Turns Itself into
The Little Shop of Horrors

Stupid PC Trick #1921

My PC did this repeatedly through the writing of this book. First, the keyboard stopped working (actually, that may have had something to do with the fact that I poked candle wax into the keys' mountings to get the keys to stop squeaking as I typed, then, when they stopped working altogether, I remounted each on safety pin heads).

Then my hard drive started making weird grinding and munching sounds before it crashed. Finally, in an occurrence too spooky to be coincidence, just as I was typing "Information Highway Tip #211B—How to Find the Communications Port," all four communications ports simultaneously self-destructed.

As a computer professional I knew exactly what to do: I heaved a coffee cup at the wall and broke a six-inch chunk out of the plaster.

After that, it was just minutes before the mouse, the motherboard, the monitor, and the new keyboard also blew.

I proceeded to spend a sleepless 36 hours struggling frantically to figure out what was wrong but to no avail. Discouraged, I spent the rest of the weekend in a gloomy funk, rapping my fingers on the computer table, calling all my friends and telling them about my miserable life.

Once again, the PC had turned itself into The Little Shop of Horrors. Like the hot-house plant of movie fame, hungry for human flesh, it was bent upon destroying my life.

When your PC turns itself into The Little Shop of Horrors, don't let it spoil your day. Go out, have a cup of cappuccino, buy yourself some expensive jewelry, ride the subway to the other side of the city just for the hell of it. When you get back to your office, jiggle the cables or search through your desk drawer for a stray chip or something. Remember, when it comes to fixing a PC, the best plan of attack is always aimlessness. You'll never be able to fix a computer by reading manuals, phoning tech support, or using logic to figure out what's wrong. PCs don't work that way. They're more like curmudgeonly great-aunts who only cooperate when the spirit moves them. Try feeding it rat poison instead.

The PC as Psychic Animal

J ust as zodiac signs can predict every nuance of human behavior, PC sun signs have proven to be remarkably accurate in forecasting reliable operation.

To help you better understand your computer's spiritual side, leading astrologers have charted these PC horoscopes. Unlike newspaper horoscopes, which are printed with a disclaimer that they should serve only as entertainment, these horoscopes are for real. You can feel confident organizing your PC's life around them. (The date corresponding to your PC's zodiac sign is the date that your computer was actually built. Call your dealer if you don't know for sure, and be sure to tell them that you need the build date in order to figure out your PC's sun sign.)

Aquarius (January 20 to February 18)

Aquarius PCs teeter between stern reliability and an obsessive belief they're a bubble gum machine. The latter is probably due to the influence of Jupiter and its penchant for spinning through space. Computers manufactured under the sign of Aquarius exert strange influences on office bottled-water dispensers. Ever wander into an office and spot a skinny-legged programmer staggering around, clenching a ten-gallon water bottle, trying futilely to change the bottle on the dispenser without spilling all the water? There's an Aquarius PC somewhere on the premises.

Pisces (February 19 to March 20)

Einstein was a Pisces and that's no surprise, because Pisces are prone to daydreaming about the shape of the universe. Should your PC gives you an error message like "Failure Writing to Drive A: Abort? Retry? Ignore?" it's not because it can't write data to the floppy drive. It's probably lost in some grand mathematical calculation about the gravitation curvature of space–time. These are very metaphysical questions, after all. Pisces PCs never work well with Aquarius ones because Aquarius PCs are suspicious of any computer that likes phrasing numerical problems in terms of the number of gumballs in a bubble gum machine.

Aries (March 21 to April 19)

PCs born under the sign of the Ram excel at looking busy when they're not. That makes them ideal machines for anyone aspiring to a managerial position. Their tendency to not suffer cataclysmic breakdowns makes them well-suited to the employee who likes to save up sick days to take mini-vacations to the Mall of America in Minnesota. Their affability makes them ideal laptop computers: They pack up quickly and conveniently into a suitcase, and they prefer not to be taken out. Be warned that the Aries PC is known for its sex drive. In some cultures, reset buttons pried off Aries computer are prized as aphrodisiacs and command a high price in the voodoo market.

Taurus (April 20 to May 20)

No machine is as bull-headed as a Taurus PC. Direct descendants of the cotton gin, Taurus PCs are known for toiling long hours in the sun without respite—and also begetting slavery. An ideal work machine? Think again. Their impatient Type-A personalities make them humorless boors with keyboards that break easily under impassioned pounding. Don't expect to fire up a game of Jane of the Jungle on a Taurus PC. Chances are you'll either get the messages "Insufficient memory" or this stubborn beast will bump you back into your marketing database where you're supposed to be. As for computer-aided design, all your drawings will come out looking like the insides of factories condemned by OSHA. If your laptop is a Taurus, expect to spend long hours with it on exotic beaches actually crunching numbers.

Gemini (May 21 to June 21)

If you've got a Gemini PC, expect a workday packed full of surprises. One minute your mercurial Gemini will be faxing a client in Hoboken, the next it will be plunging off on computer packet lines to Saudi Arabia or constructing fanciful word-processing documents explaining how the shipping and receiving department can become a world power. Life is never dull with a computer assembled under the sign of Dr. Jekyll and Ms. Hyde. Such PCs are often creatively gifted as children, and will lead you off on unexpected artistic excursions, designing multimedia gone-to-lunch notes and illustrating your memos with clip-art nuclear submarines. Be warned that their eccentricity seeps in quickly, and before long, like the Commodore Amiga, they are elderly crackpots spouting out-of-date macro strings and groaning into their oatmeal.

Cancer (June 22 to July 22)

Like the co-worker in the next cubicle who's life is but one long soliloquy of complaint, PCs that bear the sign of the Crab are prone to kvetching, luckless circumstances, and a moodiness that frequently vexes their more logical masters. Their batteries are unable to clock time accurately for more than three days. Their internal fan whines with an oblique gloom. Their disks keep returning read/write errors, even after you've run repair and diagnostics software on them for 48 hours straight. Whenever you install a new software package, the machine crashes. Sometimes, personal problems so overwhelm the Cancer PC that the only solution is to turn the machine off and leave it alone for a few days. The Cancer PC frequently requires long stretches of solitude for emotional repair.

Leo (July 23 to August 22)

You might think that having a Leo computer would guarantee you a lionly companion, but you'd be wrong. If your computer was assembled under the stars of the Lion, chances are it will regard itself not as a king, but as The King. "You ain't nothin' but a hound dog, cryin' all the time!" can be heard wafting from the speakers of a PC that comes into this world thinking it's an Elvis impersonator. "Love me tender, love me true!" it will croon disjointedly when you reconfigure its autoexec.bat file. "Don't step on those blue suede shoes!" it will howl when you try to reformat its hard disk. Your sessions at the computer will be dampened by the eerie feeling that your PC would rather be strumming an electric guitar in a second-rate teenage beach movie. Hook a microphone to it and let it wail.

Virgo (August 23 to September 22)

If your PC bears the sign of the Virgin, be warned that it is an electronic version of the ubiquitous teenager-at-the-mall. More obnoxious than innocent, more presumptuous than demure, the Virgo PC works best when a TV set is standing on the desk beside it, preferably blaring MTV. Its flagrantly disorganized subdirectories and unworkable configuration file are the PC's equivalent of nail-polished toes and a backwards baseball cap. Never saw a PC with "mall hair"? You've never seen all the gunk that static can attract to a Virgo PC's screen. Like totally awesome.

Libra (September 23 to October 23)

A PC born under the sign of the Balance is the kind of computer you want your accountant to have. Like the dour gray-flannel guy in the office at the end of the hall, who's always working hard when you pass his door, the Libra PC is a computer that's always in control. It may seem bland and emotionless most of the time, but it and its world are always in perfect working order. Should some madman slip into the outer office with a bomb, you can count on the Libra PC to quietly put aside its spreadsheet, glance up, and cooly activate the electronic lock on the doors. Libra PCs are much in demand for running nuclear weapons installations, overseeing space shuttle lift-offs, and serving as romantic adversaries in *Star Trek: Deep Space Nine*.

Scorpio (October 24 to November 21)

Scorpio computers make perfect soul mates for guys or gals who are always stirring up trouble in the office. Scorpios live to sift through heaps of innocuous data in search of that one bit of information that will stall congressional bills, derail manufacturing plans, and ultimately save the world. They are PCs best suited to social idealists, successful entrepreneurs, and others who live life on the edge. As a consequence, Scorpio PCs are often found battered and bruised, for they are often the unlucky ones who are spirited away to dark rooms and bludgeoned while their user is hiding in the cupboard. You find a lot of Scorpio PCs in second-hand computer stores. Like wrinkled peace protest banners, they sit on the shelves like relics of a forgotten spirit.

Sagittarius (November 22 to December 21)

Computers kissed by the sign of the Archer are the computer world equivalent of the long-distance athlete. They're blessed with the fastest processors, the fastest hard disks, and the slickest video. They have one flaw though: they love to sit in the pro club for hours, spinning their masculine drives, sucking in the juice, and bragging about how many disks they can fill up during a hard disk backup. The problem is Pluto. Whenever Pluto travels through Capricorn and Saturn is in the House of Hunan, Sagittarius PCs forget which device drivers are loaded and start filling up their disks with digitized pictures of Batman. The only solution is to keep the PC on a strict aerobics regimen by firing up Minesweeper once a day and playing it until the network crashes.

Capricorn (December 22 to January 19)

Computers screwed together under the troublesome sign of Capricorn are called Wicked Goats. They will eat anything—spreadsheets, databases, word processing documents, or accounting files. Type data into a Capricorn computer and you are as good as guaranteed that you will never see it again. Not only does data disappear from its memory, but it also disappears from the Capricorn PC's hard disk. And the more important the data is, the more likely it is to disappear. Have you ever installed a labyrinthine system of subdirectories on your PC's hard disk, only to find it gone the next day? You have a Capricorn PC. Owners of Capricorn PCs tend to amass every data-recovery software package available on the market. They can frequently be seen walking around, scratching their heads, saying, "But I was sure I saved that file to disk!" Pluto and Saturn in the House of Hunan are to blame.

Excuses for When You Do Something Really Stupid with a Computer

Let's face it. We all suffer embarrassing moments with our computers. You press a wrong key or kick the hard disk, and suddenly the office network has vanished. The trick is to recover gracefully, like the skater who is face down on the ice one minute and spinning a triple lutz the next. Here are some excuses to help you recover from your computer errors with aplomb.

The Experienced Fighter Pilot at the Mercy of Defective Equipment Excuse

"The machine was humming like an F-16 with lit afterburners. Stars whizzed by. The clouds whooshed by behind. Then I pressed <ctrl> <alt> <tab> and it was as if the universe itself exploded."

The Experienced Ace Computer Programmer Excuse

"No, no. I didn't do anything that I haven't done a hundred times before. Must be your computer."

The Defective Office Wiring Excuse

"Come to think of it, there have been a lot of strange occurrences in my office involving electricity lately. I think it's the wiring. Why, I bet there are millions of stray volts surging madly through the wires in my office and I don't even know it."

The Malicious Computer Virus Excuse

"You mean you haven't heard of the Electrolysis-4 MegaDeath Computer Virus?! Why, just last month it infected every major university, government installation, and Fortune 500 company. It even infected the automated teller outside my bank (the reason my football pool check bounced). No, I'm not surprised it wiped out the entire office computer network. Nor am I surprised that there's a message in the network log file that says that I was the one who accidentally typed 'DELETE *.*' in the network's root directory thus obliterating the network. That is the first symptom of the Electron-4 MegaVirus—excuse me, did I say Electron-4? I meant Electrolysis-4."

The Psychic Premonition Excuse

"So last night I had this dream that my PC was calling to me. It was calling, 'Help! I'm falling and I can't get up!' But no matter how hard I ran, I couldn't get to it in time. Then, wouldn't you know it, when I got to my office today, the PC looked like it had been beaten around the monitor with a baseball bat—as if someone was really upset with it and had done this to it."

Technology in the Year 20,000:
We Make Contact

In the year 20,000, high technology will have to fight to maintain its practical bent, despite mounting pressure from futurists for adequately futuristic frivolity. In the following prophecies on what life, science, and technology will be like millennia hence, we strive for more responsible realism.

T he year 20,000 will be a thrilling one, thanks to a long-awaited abeyance of Elvis-mania. That, and an end to riot-inducing shortages of dashboard air fresheners for space capsules will spawn a veritable golden age in human achievement.

Among the year's other landmarks: Einstein's Theory of Relativity will be replaced by double-jackpot lotto on fourteen major planets. More people than ever before will learn the difference between a digital computer and a Chinese fire drill. After one last desperate round of drug tests, the Food and Drug Administration and the National Institutes of Health will finally decree the human condition to be incurable. Rocky, desolate moons of little known planets will become hip weekend getaways for people with lots of money but little soul. Here are some other developments:

On the Little Green Neighbors Front...

Space explorers will discover that extraterrestrials don't have three noses, four toes, silver earlobes, and tails that look like Day-Glo cigars. Rather they find that they're boring little creatures who dress like accountants and eat meatloaf each night while watching *The MacNeil/Lehrer NewsHour.* When space explorers say to them, "Take me to your ruler," they reply, "I think I left it in my briefcase back at the space pod."

For the first time, physicists are struck by the horror that the universe is a much duller place than anyone ever imagined. Some will commit suicide.

On the Twelve Days of Science Front...

Through a fluke in the attendance records of the annual meeting of the Pan-Galactic Sodality of Sciences Association, it will be discovered that hypothesis is not the first bold step on the road to scientific truth, but rather a form of temporary insanity that can be cured by two vitamin-B tablets and a brisk slap on the face.

Scientific journals will be swamped with last-minute revisions that month.

Noted space–time theorist Artemus Bung will advance his theory that the universe is only as wide as the number of potato chips that it takes to spell "particle physics" across the top of one's desk. In an errata sheet attached to the end of his myth-shattering paper, he theorizes that after sipping enough schnapps, Euclid's elements become indistinguishable from the eyelashes of a certain dominatrix named Edith.

Bung is hailed as the Einstein of his age. Soon after, he wins the Nobel Prize. Potato chip sales soar. A worldwide hunt begins for Edith.

On the Techno-What? Front...

Computer superconductivity will evolve into three new charismatic religions and a double-decker bus with an especially neat racing stripe painted on its side.

On March 7, at exactly 6:32 P.M., in a university computing center poised on the edge of science history, the days when the phrase "structured computer programming" was not always considered a non sequitur will be forgotten. Once and for all. Completely. For good.

After many delays, IBM will introduce its PS/4 personal computer line. That's all, just four.

By fall, an estimated 8 million patents will have been granted for devices designed to reduce static electricity in corporate computer rooms—an occasional source of aberrant computer behavior. All of the devices will be capable of being rendered ineffectual by one big Persian cat.

On the If-You-Can't-Understand-It, Legislate-It Front...

Alarmed by the ever-increasing varieties of emerging technologies and the near-impossibility of regulating them all before they grow obsolete, world leaders band together in a frantic mass law-writing effort. They form an organization called, rather uninspiredly, The Organization of Technology (TOT). Its headquarters consist of one black rotary phone, an overworked secretary, and a broken mimeograph machine from the 20th century. It is run by a bureaucrat who is always out of town.

The only thing of consequence that TOT will ever accomplish is drafting a formidable set of regulations to legislate the placing of bumper stickers on milk shake machines. By then, milk shake machines will have been obsolete for over 8,000 years. Legislators will nonetheless decree the use of tax dollars spent on The Organization of Technology well worth it.

On the Why-Ordinary-People-Love-Technology Front...

Widespread civil unrest over an especially cryptic and unreadable computer manual will result in four days of rioting in the streets of New Delhi. Crowds will finally calm when the publisher of the manual agrees to rewrite it, making use of paragraphs and grammatically correct sentences.

The move will be hailed as a major victory for humanity and celebrated for days.

The breakup of AT&T will continue with the same fervor with which it began in the latter half of the 20th century. Federal Judge Harold H. Greene, who presided over the beginning of the breakup of AT&T in the 20th century and has been kept in suspended animation ever since, is revived every couple of millennia to announce a new ruling.

By this time, the former telecommunications giant's empire will have been reduced to one telephone pole in Namibia and a battered pay phone in back of a coffee shop in Bangor, Maine. In a last-ditch effort to reassert its corporate might, AT&T will begin secretly buying from consumers all the red phones in use. It will then proceed to buy up all the blue ones.

However, AT&T's efforts will be derailed by an ever-vigilant Judge Greene, who will be brought out of suspended animation to buy up all the green phones.

Telephone users will still be lamenting that Ma Bell was ever plucked apart in the first place, and only three people in the entire western quadrant of the Milky Way will be able to figure out their phone bills.

On the Hyperspace Trade Diplomacy Front...

When Planet Earth finds itself being tipped out of its galactic orbit by a glut of Japanese computers, Japanese TVs, Japanese VCRs, Japanese stereos, Japanese camcorders, Japanese moon shuttles, Japanese satellites, and Japanese space ports, worried environmentalists petition world leaders for emergency relief.

Typically, diplomatic world leaders respond by exiling the Japanese to their own special planet. Their planet is far, far away, tucked in a corner of the galaxy where the only thing for thousands of light years around is a big asteroid that provides extra parking for a nearby bowling alley.

Ironically, the Japanese are happy on their planet. They dub it "The Planet of the Jammed On/Off Button." For the first time since their ascendancy as the universe's consumer electronics king they have enough room to do all their shipping and invoicing.

The problem of Planet Earth being tipped out of its orbit by too much consumer electronics does not abate, however. Japanese stereos, microwaves, VCRs, and mini-cassette recorders still filter back across the galaxy. They are smuggled down to Planet Earth in greater numbers than ever before.

World leaders grow apoplectic. World leaders, however, are always apoplectic, and as usual, the apoplexy never translates into any effort to solve the problem. Another 2,000 years will pass before the problem is finally addressed. By then, Planet Earth will be circling the sun in a roller-derby heat with Uranus and Pluto.

On the Futurist Problem Front...

Following the advice of prominent world leaders, social anthropologists, newspaper advice columnists, and a lot of ordinary people who are just plain fed up, every self-proclaimed futurist who has ever gone on record as predicting a day when we all will inhabit wheel-shaped pink homes in the sky and ride to the local shopping mall on the tails of four-toed aliens will be rounded up and placed in the back of an old station wagon. The station wagon will be driven down a deserted road, parked, and forgotten.

The population of Planet Earth will breath a sigh of relief that it is finally free of fanciful-brained futurists.

Unfortunately, come nightfall, the station wagon will be discovered by a roving band of stereo headphone smugglers. They will take the futurists with them to the Planet of the Jammed On/Off Button.

There the futurists will be fed, clothed, housed, and put to work running the Japanese's catalog outlet centers. As usual, the Japanese will prove themselves to be cleverer than the rest of the universe.

From *The Secret Programmer's Handbook, vers. 12899.586b*

The following is from a page found crumpled between old newspapers used as packing in a shipment of software that arrived recently at a Fortune 500 company. The page was ripped from a book that many computer programmers have heard of, but most will claim doesn't actually exist. This apocryphal book allegedly reveals all the sneaky tricks that software developers use to make their customers think that their software is working when there's no guarantee that it is. According to urban myth, the book has gone through so many revisions that people are starting to mistake it for a computer operating system. The book has been banned in Toronto.

Program the software to beep whenever you want to reassure the user that the software is responding to their input in a suitable fashion. It is not necessary that the software actually be responding.

It is important to program the software to beep only when good things happen. Don't let the software beep when bad things happen.

If the program is taking too long to do something, put something on the user's screen—a picture of an hourglass perhaps, or a clock. Even a blank box will do. People tend to forget that they're waiting too long for something when you put something on their screen.

Let users use their mouse with the software as much as possible, even when there's no need to use a mouse. This will cut down on calls to tech support. People tend to think something's wrong with the software when they can't use their mouse.

To make the user feel in control, let them adjust the program's colors. Users like to adjust colors, even when they're not in control.

Give them at least three colors to adjust. Make one of them blue.

Never make the software's main screen perfectly symmetrical. Users are suspicious of perfectly symmetrical computer screens. If two columns of items are listed on a screen, don't align them. Instead, make one list appear longer than the other.

Never put too much information on any single program screen. It causes users, especially the bright ones, to panic.

Put lots of pictures on the first screen of the software, especially if the program is buggy. Users tend to be more favorably disposed toward software if it gives them pleasing pictures to look at. They may even forget that it's buggy. They'll think, "O.K., so the software doesn't work right, but at least it gives me a nice picture of the Statue of Liberty, plus one of the Piazza Del Rio to look at."

Never Log On to Anything with the Name "Bambi"

Information Highway Tip #368

Do not answer E-mail from strangers whose computer logon might be interpreted as a slang term for teenage boys who have not been circumcised. If you are unsure of what this slang term might be, play it safe. Do not answer E-mail from any stranger whose computer logon name sounds like the name of a vegetable, rhymes with "Rambo," or reminds you in any way of a specimen pictured in a textbook for a public health course. Make exceptions for people whom you suspect might represent your congressional district in public office.

Gadget Lust

One man's story of how his life was destroyed
by an addiction to high-tech toys.

P racticality had nothing to do with it. It was more pri-
mal than that. It was instinctual, pulling Oscar against
his will, over his protestations, to the computer store sales
counter where he gurgled like an addict, "Gimme!" then
whipped out a credit card.

His wife was determined that he take this latest purchase back. But he pointed out that $1,899 was a small price
to pay for peace of mind. He chucked aside the sponge
packing and pulled out the cardboard. Still, it really was a
small price to pay for happiness.

Oscar marched down the basement stairs with the
Electro-Pooket in his arms, beaming. He could hear his wife
calling after him, "It's a sickness! We can get you a doctor!"
But there was little chance of either rehabilitation or even
marginal cure. His MasterCard's credit limit was too high,
and, thanks to his living next to a transformer tower, the
amp service to his house was high enough to power a small
industrial nation, so the number of appliances he could plug
into the outlets was nearly limitless.

Oscar positioned the Electro-Pooket lovingly on a
worktable amid all the other electronic devices he had purchased while gripped by the throes of gadget lust. He
switched it on. He stepped back to let the glow of the monitor sweep over him, to bathe him in phosphorescent Eden

green. His heart thrilled, his brain drummed. It was almost as good as free-basing state-of-the-art stereo components.

He had been lucky. For most of his life he had been able to nurture his gadget lust discreetly. His wife never questioned the number of electronics catalogs that arrived in the mail by the kilo each month, wrapped in brown paper sleeves and which pandered to people with electrical engineering degrees who were under the care of the state.

The salesclerks at the electronics stores Oscar frequented never complained about the furtive looking man with VCR set-up directions dangling from his hip pocket, who paced the aisles of their stores almost every night, zombie-like, covetously caressing programmable phones and demanding more high-performance features from his clock radios than normal men did.

Oscar's friends knew about his problem, of course. Many suffered the same affliction. With basement rec rooms cluttered with computers and tangled with wiry effluvium, their lives were one long string of visits to the local Radio Shack for batteries, cables, or audio plugs. Wherever they went, they left behind them rolls of electrical tape, and every fuse seller in the city knew them by their first names.

Often their spouses never suspected a thing—until the later stages of the disease, anyway. Oscar's own wife didn't suspect a thing until one weekend when they were picnicking in the vicinity of an especially large radio transmitter tower. She had just spread the blanket on the ground when she spotted her husband climbing the radio tower, King Kong fashion. "I want it!" Oscar bleated. "I need it! Don't worry, I can make it fit in the basement!"

It took two park rangers and a St. Bernard the rest of the afternoon to coax him down. On the way home he suffered a relapse upon spotting a satellite dish propped in the front yard of a farm along the highway. "I want it! I must have it!" he whimpered, until his wife pulled the car to the side of the road and let him fling himself into the dish with abandon.

Several weeks later, when they lost their two children in a maze of stacks of old issues of *Popular Electronics*, his wife decided that the time had come to seek professional help.

According to Professor Thomas J. Dimsdale of the University of Boorslag, an internationally known expert on eroto-gadgetism, victims typically pass through three stages. In the first stage, sufferers become adept at translating any dollar amount into the amount of computer equipment it will buy them. For instance, $150 translates into four lithium batteries, an RS-232 breakout box, a diskette organizer, and one 150-watt power supply upgrade. Two hundred dollars becomes a portable IC tester, a cable gender changer, a pilot-style joystick, a two-in-one screwdriver, and a AA battery.

In the second stage, sufferers become indifferent to the threat of electrical shock while futzing with a treasured appliance. "Don't worry, I've been knocked unconscious by house current lots of times" is a frequently heard comment. Another good tip-off is the remark, "What's the fuss? I've already lost the skin on the upper half of my body twice to radio-frequency burns."

The third and final stage is marked by the sufferer's smiling with sublime pleasure whenever the alarm on their digital watch sounds. The most that friends and loved ones can do at this stage is to wipe the drool from the victim's face whenever he spots any electronic gizmo more whizbang than anything he owns.

Oscar fell asleep content that night, knowing that the monkey within was placated for the moment. The Electro-Pooket, with its shimmering buttons, lights, indicators, keys, and switches was enthroned in the rec room like Eden rebuilt with state-of-the-art transistors. Had he not purchased that chip bloated Jezebel, he would have been guaranteed a night of pacing the floor, hollow-eyed, fumbling through the tatters of electronics magazine ads in his bathrobe pockets, crying out for technology so shiny and state-of-the-art, captured by the greedy arms of gadget lust.

Instead, Oscar had new buttons to play with, new cables to untangle, new switches to futz with, and new documentation to unfurl and wonder over. This was heaven.

Your Cat's Guide
to Your Computer

Cats are using computers more and more these days. As it turns out, computers are the perfect objects to sit on, rub up against, spit fur balls on, muck up with cat hair, and hiss at.

Forget the sewing basket with the spools of thread. Forget the laundry hamper with shreddable pantyhose. Computers are much more attractive. What more could a cat want than floppy disks to trounce, monitors to scratch, mouse pads to claw, and laser printers for yoga or acrobatics practice. And, unlike the common stereo or TV, computers have lots of sensitive electronic components that can be rendered inoperable by a single cat hair. And, unlike rats, squirrels, or gophers, computers don't fight back.

Computers hold other advantages for cats. Consider the prestige factor. Simply sit in front of one for a long time without moving and people will think you are a very smart dude. Try sitting like that in front of the refrigerator and people will start making jokes about you.

Cats adapt naturally to computers. Millions of years of evolutionary pressures have led to cats' perfecting sophisticated survival skills that enable them to sit for long hours without moving on top of a piece of consumer electronics, like a TV. (Humans, in contrast, sit in front of the TV set. You can see how far our evolutionary mechanisms have gotten us.) The leap from TV top to computer is an easy one for most cats to make. In fact, few cats ever notice any difference between the two, especially if humans are staring zombie-eyed at both. However, few make the leap without pulling the lamp along with them.

Not surprisingly, a good portion of the Information Highway is devoted to cats, their worship, their maladies, their whims, their wit, and even (how could we forget?) their intelligence. (In contrast, the portion of the Information Highway devoted to dogs is usually gloomy with E-mail about how dogs like to roll in horse dung and snort.) The mission of the Information Highway is, of course, to celebrate the cerebral and artistic things in life, and what could be more cerebral and artistic than a cat who doesn't fall off a computer or a TV?

If cats could write computer books, they would surely have a lot to tell us about these brutish machines with an insufficient amount of body fur to be truly stylish. Here are a few tips from Kitty.

Maintaining Your Dignity in Front of a Computer

Remember that you are a creature of beauty and intelligence. If the computer fails to cooperate, simply sigh and turn your head away ever so slowly. Maintain your dignity at all costs.

Flip your tail at the computer's screen if it fails to adequately acknowledge your regal presence. Then gnaw its electrical cords.

Never sit on top of the monitor. You may fall off. But do make sure to drop as much cat litter into its vents as possible.

Never eat shrink-wrap. It's too hard to digest. Try disk labels instead.

Never stick your nose inside a printer that goes "clack-clack" when it's going "clack-clack."

Only walk over the keyboard when you have fresh cat litter between your toes.

When spitting up fur balls, always do so behind the computer where no one will find them.

If the computer gives you a hard time, tear its plastic face off (you know, the one that lists the model number). Bat it around the floor. Then eat it.

While dropping a dead mammal on the keyboard when someone is typing usually never fails to elicit some type of response, most humans will misinterpret the action. They will think you are offering them a token of affection, when what you are actually trying to tell them is that they should stop fooling around with the computer and go hunt for small rodents before they and their family starve.

Never underestimate the power of stepping on some-one when they're trying to use that stupid computer. Should they try to remove you from their lap, grab a lampshade with one paw, flail your back feet in their face, and mew your heart out. Eventually they will return you to their lap. They will apologize, pet you, and feel guilty for having taken you from your mother at such an early age.

Don't let a human con you into thinking it's O.K. to stroke you with one hand while typing on the computer with the other. You want to be stroked with both hands! You are a direct descendant of the Egyptian cat-goddess Bastet and deserve no less. Should they persist in giving you only half their attention, rise up on your hind legs and position yourself so that your body obstructs their reach of the keyboard. Flap your tail in their face to make sure that they devote their full attention to you.

If all else fails, walk on the keyboard.

Debunking Myths About Computers

Contrary to rumor, no one has ever lost a tail in a disk drive door.

If people warn you that your hair is apt to short out the computer, ignore them. If it does, someone will fix it. If they don't, who cares?

So what if a computer can perform 8 million mathematical calculations each second? You can sleep for 16 hours straight in a computer box. I ask you, who is the superior being?

Unlike cats, computers are not perfect.

The barbarism of these machines is evidenced by the fact that there is no place in, on, or around the computer that has been designed to take a nap in.

Computers may be from a different planet, but remember that you are too, and you got here first.

A computer mouse isn't.

Never Write E-mail Messages with Too Many \<smirk\> \<smirk\>, \<snicker\> \<snicker\>s

I knew a poor fellow from South Carolina who had a problem shared with the folks who performed with Monty Python. Whenever he typed a public E-mail message on a computer bulletin board, it was invariably riddled with \<he-he\>s, \<smirk\>s, \<snicker\>s, \<guffaw\>s and \<haw-haw!\>s. The messages themselves were harmless. He would write things like "My grandpa had this chicken \<he-he\> \<snicker\>." And, "So the turtle and the tortoise are walking down a road, and the turtle says to the tortoise \<wink\> \<snicker\>..."

The \<snicker\> \<snicker\>s, \<guffaw\>s, and \<smirk\>s enraged the feminists on the board. It wasn't the messages' contents they found offensive, but all the snickering that was going on. The \<wink\>s especially irritated them.

Finally, after one excessively \<snicker\>-laden message, the women exploded.

"Take your <wink> <wink>, <snicker> <snicker>s outta here before I blow your head off!" one blasted. Another grumbled, "This is a respectable BBS frequented by many respectable business women!!! [Her exclamation points.] If I wanted to get <wink><winked>, <snicker> <snickered>, I'd go to a redneck bar."

So the fellow from South Carolina disappeared into the bitstream. Like many such typographically effusive men, he had struggled mightily to fulfill the female mandate that men more freely share their deepest emotions, but he was crucified when he did.

"We Are All Connected" Means
More Than You Think

I have never admitted this to anyone before. I would surely never admit it to any of my professional peers. But I can't get my fax-modem to work.

A fax-modem is a palm-sized device that in some incarnations looks like an electronic stun gun, and in others like a brutal chunk of electronics that looks capable of blowing up foreign airports.

It is attached to a computer, usually by a long black cable of the sort that you might see snaking in aimless heaps around the ankles of heavy-metal guitarists. The idea is that with the fax-modem you send and receive faxes with your computer. The fax-modem comes into your computer via a phone line, and it exits via a phone line. That's the idea anyway. It's just like something out of James Bond.

Unfortunately, I can't get mine to work. Whenever a fax wants to come into my computer, the phone rings, the lights on the modem flicker in a propitious way, but the computer remains inert. Sometimes it makes a series of clicking sounds like the sound of an FBI phone tap, the tiny picture of the fax-modem at the bottom of the computer screen shivers, then the computer and the fax-modem both go completely dead.

I would tell everyone to stop trying to send me faxes and send all their communiqués via U.S. mail instead, if it weren't for one thing: I'm supposed to be some sort of expert on getting faxes to work. You see, I write a magazine column in which I answer readers' letters describing their troubles with their computers. Specifically, I provide advice on getting a computer to pick up the phone and talk to other computers. It is kind of a Dear Abby column, except that most of the letters I receive these days concern fax-modems. The letters arrive in big bundles via U.S. mail, and not by fax, for obvious reasons.

A typical letter will begin, "I own a brand-new V-Bus Micro-Mini Computer with a 48256 Socket, eight parallel ports, seven UARTS, a DIP bank, programmable buttons, a full range of connectors, 80 megahertz cold fusion bus, add-on cards, built-in memory... etc." This description of hardware will wind down to the end of the page. There it will end abruptly, "...and it doesn't work."

Sometimes the letter writer will include descriptions of other pieces of office equipment they can't get to work either, just in case I can provide any insight into this dysfunction too. Like photocopy machines. Or Teletypes. Or office phone systems. Sometimes they send me printouts of computer programs they wrote, explaining "I wrote this in GWBasic, but it won't work," as if I can really do something about it. Other times they mail me drawings of their office's floor plan, illustrating where the broken computer is located, where the broken photocopier sits, where to find the closet that houses the balky phone system. Scribbled ink lines show all the cables snaking between them.

The letters come from as far away as Pakistan, Argentina, Turkey, even Russia. At first I was surprised to see that some of these countries had faxes and computers, but I have long since learned that no one is safe. The letters from former Soviet republics are the saddest. They request that if I can't solve their computer networking woes, maybe I can instead ask my "chiefs" to send them baby food. I get lots of mail from United Nations offices too. They seem to be suffering a lot of computer networking woes between and within their far-flung agencies.

In the glimpse of the growing free world that these tragic soliloquies provide, I see humanity united not by democracy, nor by capitalism, nor even by the ability to empathize with the common struggles of man, but in the futile struggles of offices to get their fax and photocopy machines working properly.

Unlike Dear Abby, I cannot just tell everyone who writes to go get counseling (although some I do). In fact, I will probably not be able to help any of them at all.

I must tell you about one particularly troubling situation. Yesterday I received a letter from an architect in Kansas. He described how he was slumped over his computer keyboard, drained of all hope that he could ever bask in the glories of the Information Highway. He had been trying to do something that should have been very simple: send documents that he had composed in his word processor as E-mail.

This architect's quest for information on how to accomplish this seemingly mundane chore had resulted in an unbelievable two-month odyssey. With dogged determination, he had spent hours on the phone with the technical support departments of CompuServe and America Online, written all the major computer magazines, posted pleas for help on online services (where I first encountered him), and wasted many Saturday afternoons reading computer manuals that couldn't have been more poorly written had they been French crepe recipes tapped out by monkeys.

"I have to stop the pain and bleeding," his letter began. I thought he was being overly emotional (as architects often are).

Of course I'd like to help this poor man, especially since that's my job as a Computer Dear Abby. But the fact is that there's not a lot I can do for him. It seems that he has a basic misunderstanding of the principle of the fax-modem. His letter explained how he had buried his fax-modem in the cement foundation supporting a mini-mall in Cleveland. The problem is that he wants me to respond by fax.

Martyred on the Office
Computer Network

No great movement in history is without its heroes and victims, and the computer communications revolution is no exception. Whether exploring the enigmas of Internet or helping a friend get his computer to work, every participant is a hero in her own way.

Shirley Forester, Age 42, Claims Examiner, Lacunae Life & Casualty

On the afternoon of December 16, 1992, Shirley Forester vanished from sight while using her personal computer to access a casualty claims database on the office computer network.

A co-worker, on spotting Shirley's empty chair, hurried over to her desk and turned off her computer—to save power, he later claimed. It was a mistake that would haunt him for the rest of his life.

Several moments later, while strolling back to his own desk, this particular co-worker realized the gravity of what he had just done. He had erased all evidence of Shirley, as well as any hope of rescuing his colleague. At that he gasped, "Good heavens! Shirley just got sucked into the office computer network!"

Other co-workers rushed to the scene.

He explained to them what had happened. He told them that Shirley had vanished into the network, but no one believed him. They walked away, shaking their heads in disbelief and pitying this poor madman. Some left Post-It notes for Shirley to call them when she returned. They needed to warn her about her crazy colleague.

The sad fact is that Shirley Forester was never heard from again.

It is said, though, that sometimes late at night, during moments of inactivity on the insurance company network, you can catch flickers of Shirley—a sprinkle of static outlining a pince-nez, a spray of pixels suggesting a beaded sweater. Even the faint odor of cheap perfume.

The company that maintains the office computer network maintains that it's only "fuzzy coaxial." But then... when are they ever right? They can hardly keep the network from crashing.

And anyway, we know the truth.

The Bug-Feature Conversion Chart

Computer users too frequently are unable to tell the difference between a computer bug and computer feature. This convenient chart has been designed to help you distinguish easily between the two.

E ver notice how hard it can be to tell a computer bug from a valuable computer product feature? Ever spend hours on the phone, waiting on hold with a computer manufacturers' technical support department, only to be told that the bug you thought was ruining your work and your data was actually an important product feature?

How embarrassing! That is why the Bug-Feature Conversion Chart has been designed—to spare you the humiliation and wasted time of phoning tech support when your bug is in reality a feature.

Listed across the top of the chart you'll see common consumer gripes about their computers. Listed down the side are the likely technical explanations. To determine what computer product feature corresponds with your bug, locate the bug in the top row of the chart and place a finger on it. Now take another finger and place it in the left column on the technical explanation for the bug that you received from your manufacturer's tech support department. Now trace the finger on the bug down the column, while simultaneously moving the finger on the technical explanation across the row until both intersect. The square where they intersect is the product feature your bug represents.

Common Consumer Complaints About PCs Wrongly Assumed to Be Computer Bugs

You Call to Complain About This

Tech Support Tells You This

	Your PC is threatening to nuke Pittsburgh again	**Your PC's screen looks like it was caught in crossfire in a confetti war**	**The hard disk sounds like a satanic sales motivation tape played backwards**
"Leprechauns ran off with the PC's arithmetic logic unit in the middle of the night, but this is not a problem because…"	"Your PC has been designed for use in touchy diplomatic situations"	"Your PC is given to madcap adventures"	"Your PC will warn you about the leprechauns"
"There's an aerobic workout video jammed in your PC's internal expansion slot, but this is not a problem because…"	"Robert Ludlum plots have been conveniently programmed into read-only memory"	"Your PC's high-resolution graphics will work in the presence of both VHS and beta video standards"	"Your PC enjoys making human-like grunts when performing pelvic twists"
"Your fax-modem is caught in an interstellar time warp, but this is not a problem because…"	"Your PC was originally designed for long space flights but was found to work in many business situations as well"	"Complex business graphics are a snap with your PC's unique device driver"	"Your PC makes merry, chirping sounds when cleaning up after itself after someone has gotten their fingers or toes too close to the disk drive door"
"The Band-Aid must have fallen off the motherboard, but this is not a problem because…"	"Your PC has a bold and complex vision"	"The special silicon inside your PC is a testament to the human mind"	"Maintenance procedures are a snap when you use nail polish"
"Your communications port must have been thrown from your car, but this is not a problem because…"	"This is one graphical user-interface whose error messages are not given to mawkish sentimentality"	"You won't need a graphics board because your PC will keep you entertained without one"	"Your PC has a love relationship with the communications port and senses intuitively when it's in danger"
"Your microchip's mouth is full of peanut butter, but this is not a problem because…"	"Your PC excels at tasks that involve complex decision making"	"Computer simulation of the psychological problems of co-workers is a snap with the unique graphical user-interface"	"Your PC will conveniently warn you when you have run out of peanut butter"
"Your PC's central processing unit fell in the bathtub, but this is not a problem because…"	"Your PC has been specially engineered to respond to crisis"	"Your computer monitor makes a festive flotation device"	"Waterlogged floppy disk drive read-write heads can double as a loofah sponge"

Your PC Tries to Play with Your Mind by Acting Like Your Ex-Spouse

Stupid PC Trick #267

First, the PC begs you to take it along on a business trip. But once you get it on the plane, it starts complaining, spitting out disks, and acting like a brat. When you ask the PC to do something it doesn't want to, it gives you the exact same excuses that your ex-spouse would have. They are:

- Cannot read drive a: Abort? Retry? Ignore?

- Fatal error in cluster 3: Restart application

- Can't find system disk. Please insert disk that is not non-system

What to do? First of all, do not throw a scene. (The PC is hoping you will so other passengers will feel sorry for it and it will be moved to its own seat.) Instead, quietly call the flight attendant. Ask him or her if it would be possible to schedule an emergency landing of the plane. Explain that it is very important. Explain that you want to pummel the PC witless at the end of a deserted runway and leave it for dead. You want to leave it on the tarmac so that a Lufthansa airplane can run over it on its flight to Gdansk. If the attendant is at all compassionate, the flight crew will readily agree to your request.

Talk to Your PC and Other Tips
to Make It Grow

Sensitive computer components, like sensitive people, need TLC. This tutorial will help you get the most out of your PC and peripherals by keeping them in tip top shape. Read all instructions before proceeding.

T he other day, while removing a pile of dead leaves and soda cans from around my PC's central processing unit, a co-worker asked me my secrets for keeping my computer working and helping it to grow. Flattered that someone would consider my advice worth following, I reflected for a moment then scribbled the following list onto the flap of an empty fertilizer bag:

Proper mulching

Adequate shade and ventilation

Strict adherence to growing season as determined by your USDA climate zone

Pruning to remove fast-growing suckers

Weekly sprays of Carbaryl to keep flying insects out of disk drives

Avoid mutations by keeping PC from pollinating with un-desirable computers in mid-level management offices

Every experienced computer user has his or her own little secrets for bringing a PC to the peak of free-flowering perfection. The coffee grounds worked into the dirt around my desk, the daily soakings with the hose around sundown, the mounding of soil around the computer chassis to keep it moist—all these things are part of my PC maintenance ritual. And yes, dear friends, like all great gardeners, I talk to my PC. I share with it my hopes, my dreams, my musings on the mysteries of life, as well as an occasional verse from Keats, and it rewards me by not falling over into the mud as frequently as most PCs.

There is one product I would like to mention that is central to my PC-nurturing routines. That is the indestructible Data-Vac. Five pounds of vacuum cleaning brawn with a shoulder strap and crevice attachment, the Data-Vac is to motherboard dust bunnies what thermonuclear weapons are to carbon-based life forms. Imagine, if you can, a fuzz-suction animal that rumbles as loud as a city recycling truck as you and it move from laser printer to fax-modem, sucking up lint, paper clips, rubber bands, pizza, pot shards, coffee grinds, cigar butts, parking tickets, and any other office offal that could clog sensitive electronic pores and render your computer inoperable.

A $5 can of compressed air would work just as well as the Data-Vac in blowing dust out of the PC. But I ask you, does a can of compressed air come with a bag full of attachments? Can a can of compressed air be plugged into a wall outlet? Can a can of compressed air thunder like a cement mixer falling down a volcano as it goes about its work? No on all counts.

All things considered, the Data-Vac has certainly changed my life. I feel less grungy just knowing it's in the closet. Should my graphics board become gooked up with dead bugs, should my communications port become clogged with dog hair and my 25-pin connectors twisted up with old rubber bands, I know that the situation isn't hopeless. I have only to plug in the Data-Vac, snap on the dust brush, and let 'er rip. And once a day I go over all of my disk drives with the crevice tool, a sponge mop, and a bucket of Janitor in a Drum.

Top Ten Things That People Say to Their Computers When They're Alone at Night

W e share a special bond with our computers. There is no other piece of consumer electronics, with the exception of a color TV, that it is so easy to build and maintain intimacy with. A computer will listen to your problems with the patience of a 900-number fantasy friend. It will respond with the predictability of a TV remote channel changer. A computer is at once fiery and supplicating, mischievous and satisfyingly predictable. Like pets and mail-order brides, you can tell a computer anything and it has no choice but to believe you. Better, unlike the aforementioned pets and brides, a computer can never decide you're a crackpot and leave you. Here are the top ten things that people say to their computer when they're alone at night and no one can hear.

10. "<expletive deleted> <expletive deleted> <expletive deleted> <expletive deleted> <expletive deleted> <expletive deleted> <expletive deleted> <expletive deleted> <expletive deleted> snot for monkey brains!"

9. "<expletive deleted> <expletive deleted> lunatic <expletive deleted> your math coprocessor swinging by a bedsheet <expletive deleted> they'll think it's suicide!"

8. "<expletive deleted> twenty minutes to update a screen! <expletive deleted> enema bag <expletive deleted> elephant!"

7. "<expletive deleted> or you'll be tossed <expletive deleted> with the grass clippings and the old Apple IIs!"

6. "<expletive deleted> <expletive deleted> fossilized <expletive deleted> Big Foot <expletive deleted> skin lice <expletive deleted> and scabs <expletive deleted>!"

5. "Yeah, right, <expletive deleted> 'Insert Disk in Drive C.' <expletive deleted> why don't you just change your screen saver to say <expletive deleted>?!"

4. "<expletive deleted>happens to computers in communist countries <expletive deleted> reverse-engineered McDonald's cash register <expletive deleted>!"

3. "<expletive deleted> watermelon brain <expletive deleted> <expletive deleted> before you're <expletive deleted> food processor <expletive deleted> the cold waters of Boston harbor!"

2. "<expletive deleted> <expletive deleted> <expletive deleted> or you'll be stamping nine-digit zipcodes on 800 pounds of feed catalogs!"

1. "<expletive deleted> <expletive deleted> over-priced bird feeder!"

Young Technologies Fall Prey to Charming, Crusading Devil

T here is a special demon in hell. His skills are unique, his business acumen as sharply honed as that of an evil magician. His talents are legendary throughout the tinderboxes of Hades for they have been sharpened through practice since the dawn of western industrialization. His name is Abigor Pandemonium. He is a toothy rapscallion with flashy gold cufflinks, an untrustworthy grin, and the wild eyes of an idealist. His job is to infiltrate young industries and lead their products on a wild inexorable plunge from high quality into clunky tawdriness.

He was recently scheduled to give an interview to *People* magazine, but the magazine broke its appointment with Abigor. They ran in its place a 12-page photo essay by a Pulitzer prize-winning photojournalist on celebrity living rooms (the publishing industry was a recent victim of Abigor's talents), so he has consented to let the interview run here.

Interviewer: *Tell me, how did you get this job of wrecking prosperous industries? And how did you decide to put your talents to work on the computer industry?*

Abigor: First, I would like to make it clear that I do not wreck industries. I merely show the participants the quickest route to greed and self-indulgence. They do the rest. I serve as a consultant in the process. I work out of my home in the prestigious Seventh Ring of Hell. I make it a policy never to attend any stockholders' meetings if I can help it.

But how did I get this job? I spotted a classified ad in our local Seventh Ring shopper, right next to an ad for ointment to turn liver spots into a profitable home business. It said "Demon Wanted, Potential for Eternal Chaos High." That was enough for me.

Things were slow at first. I hung around watching the Industrial Revolution for about a hundred years or so. There were lots of opportunities for making mischief in mills and canning plants, but nothing that would make a young demon stand out, since the times were so tumultuous to begin with. Then I got my first break. It came when television was born.

Interviewer: *What was it about television that made it such an easy target?*

Abigor: The fact that TV had such enormous potential for creating so much good in human society. That together with the fact that enormous profits could be earned from it, made it an easy mark for corruption. Here you had these fairly inexpensive boxes that you could use to broadcast into millions of homes Shakespeare plays, Mahler symphonies, and stirring speeches that would lead entire civilizations down the path to liberty and freedom. You could train millions of people in new skills. You could teach science and mathematics. You could teach people ethics and inspire them to love one another. You could help them understand other peoples and the world around them—

Interviewer: *Just like the potential of the Information Highway to bless humankind with the free flow of knowledge and ideas?*

58

Abigor: That's right. All this incredible potential! I couldn't stand it. I knew I had to do something fast.

Interviewer: *So you subverted the promise of television by convincing TV executives to aim for profits rather than quality?*

Abigor: No, I wish I'd thought of that. Actually, I wrote a script for a sitcom pilot. It was called Evil Does Not Have Roller Skates. It was rejected by so many production companies I don't even want to think about it. I think it was ahead of its time. I eventually got jobs writing for a couple of comedy shows. I even got to produce a pilot for a sitcom once. It was called Wild Beach Bungalows of Abaddon, but it was canned because too much of the dialogue was in Latin. It didn't matter though, because the TV industry by then had outgrown its early idealistic days of striving for quality programming. The broadcast industry, in its lust for profits, was cruising the commuter lane to corporate damnation faster than any industry I had ever seen. Everywhere you turned, quality was being steam-rolled in the mad rush to humongous profits. Any hope for quality programming in the 20th century quickly grew as dim as the prospect of getting the Devil himself to tone up with a Solo-Flex.

Interviewer: *So after that you proceeded to the car industry?*

Abigor: No, I didn't think I was ready yet. I first wanted to hone my skills a little more, so I hit the household appliances industry. You know, toasters, can openers, electric knife sharpeners, coffee makers. At the time—and this was back in the '50s—all these products were rococo with chrome, leaden as boat anchors, and packed with motors more powerful than those in a lunar landing vehicle. They would last a lifetime—two if you kept them dusted.

At first, I wasn't sure what to do about the small appliance industry. It seemed almost impervious to moral corruption, so ridden was it with hoary, idealistic old men who'd gotten their start reading *Popular Mechanics*. Many first-generation industries are this way.

Then inspiration dawned: combine lightweight plastics with overseas production, sell out the original manufacturers to lackadaisical corporate conglomerates, and retire the idealistic old men to Palm Beach. Almost overnight America and much of the rest of the industrialized world was awash in flimsy plastic gewgaws that can self-destruct in a drawer of spoons.

It was a heady time. Buoyed with self-confidence, I moved on to the car industry. The same technique worked there, but with even more dramatic effect because that industry was sufficiently aged. Its original innovators were by then nothing but names behind geraniums on family plots in Grosse Point, Michigan. Its second- and third-generation inheritors were superficial enough to think that only profits move an industry.

Interviewer: *Which industries are you working on now?*

Abigor: I'm almost done with the aircraft industry. They were an especially tough nut to crack until the government got rid of airline fare price controls and foreign-government subsidized competition moved in. The telephone industry should be the next to fall. Right now they are all agog over fiber optics and super-miniaturized computer chips, but let one of them succumb to selling unwitting consumers low-priced trash, and soon that's what everyone will be selling if it means more lucre. It's already happening to the computer industry. You're starting to see a lot of computer companies whose names were once synonymous with quality running screaming ads with clowns and parachuters on late-night TV. That's what I like to see: the ads that scream "Lowest Prices in Town! We're Priced to Move Truckloads!"

Interviewer: *So tell me about your plans for the Information Highway.*

Abigor: Actually, I'm not going to have to do much. The process is already rolling, thanks to the groundwork I laid with the television, publishing, and appliance industries. Humans have surprised even me with how quick they've been to size up this Information Highway gig in terms of dollars rather than social good. It's inspiring [He snickers, cracking his knuckles.] —even to a hoary cynic like me. I predict that it won't be long before this so-called Information Highway is nothing but a handful of worthless databases full of *USA Today* weather maps. Sure, the price of access will drop, as have the prices of all the other brave new technologies, but the value and information content will fall and fall until—

[His fingers tap the desk, making the pinging sound of something falling into a great, dark depth.]

Interviewer: *And you see no hope at all?*

Abigor: If I could see hope, do you think I'd be as powerful as I am? Think about it: newspapers are a quarter of the size they were a half century ago. Encyclopedias are half as large. Computer dictionaries contain a fraction of the number of words as the one on your desk. TV news tells you less than news on the radio, and the radio offers less than the newspaper. Technology doesn't expand the information you receive, foolish man, but shrinks it. The way I see it, the Information Highway will give man a more constricted view of his world than he thinks he has, plus his chances of attaining real knowledge will be less than at any other time in history.

Interviewer: *Do you have one secret of your success you'd like to share?*

Abigor: First, let an industry's founders die off. Those are the ones who always seem to suffer a fixation on making their products high-quality. Then move in on the heirs like a cagey lawyer. Tell them to cheapen their products, cut wages, cut employee benefits, turn the factories into sweatshops, abandon quality craftsmanship, lower their prices, scrap all their research projects, then watch as the industry destroys itself with greed. [He laughs.] It's a simple formula, isn't it?

Interviewer: *Thank you, Abigor. We will honor your request and not publish your Internet E-mail address.*

Do Not Start Flame Wars

A flame war is what happens when you post an E-mail message on a public information system like Internet or CompuServe, saying something that offends people. In response, massive numbers of offended people will write you messages that are designed to offend you, then massive numbers of offended people write them messages that are designed to offend them. You get the point. Before long the whole information service looks like a Donnybrook Fair.

Here are the phrases most apt to incite flame wars. These flame wars will escalate to such a degree that large portions of the In-formation Highway will need to be shut 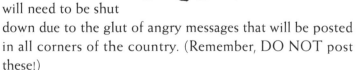 down due to the glut of angry messages that will be posted in all corners of the country. (Remember, DO NOT post these!)

"[Insert name of your least favorite NFL team] is the worst football team that has ever existed."

"Star Trek *is stupid. It is far less intellectually challenging than old* episodes of Lost in Space *starring June Lockhart and Billy Mumy."*

"The programming language C is not hard to learn. In fact, like most programming languages, it was designed for simpletons. Any dope can master it in their spare time."

"I love/hate Rush Limbaugh."

"I do/do not believe in aliens."

Remember, DO NOT post these! Unless, of course, your E-mail algorithm curve has begun to sag.

The PC Turns Your Car into a Private Pleasure Palace

Stupid PC Trick #98

L ike a dog or small child, a personal computer should never be left alone in a car, especially on hot days. But not because the PC may be kidnapped or die of heat exhaustion. Rather it is because your PC knows things about the world that you do not. Like what a "bubble sort" is and where its serial port is located. Because PCs know these things, they are also fully capable of turning on the ignition and jerking the car backward and forward in your parking space until they puke. (Luckily, few of them know how to drive a stick shift.)

To spare yourself this public embarrassment, take these precautions:

- Never drive your PC anywhere in a mini-van. Megalomaniacs like mini-vans, and so do PCs. Mini-vans have lots of room and, given enough space, your PC may very well decide it's a Zamboni machine, or worse, a hot sandwich dispenser. Then what will become of your spreadsheets?

- Always make sure that the PC is firmly buckled in with a lap belt. The last thing you want while cruising down the freeway is for the PC to get loose and start pulling on your hair or demanding that you stop for hot dogs.

- If you have a portable television in the car, do not let the PC watch it while you're away from the car. Especially do not let it watch *This Old House*. PCs that have been left alone watching *This Old House* have been known to tear out the back seat and replace it with poorly attached Corinthian molding.

How to Safely Upgrade Your Computer to Keep Up with the Rest of the Information Highway Drivers Speeding By

L ike childbirth, upgrading a computer's hardware and software is something that most people swear they will never do a second time. Things break, nothing works, directions are muddled, you call the manufacturer's tech support line and are put on hold for the rest of the day. Inevitably, an upgrade you planned to do in an afternoon takes at least thirty days.

Why do computer owners endure upgrades time and again? Because PCs keep changing. Last year's hot-rod spreadsheet cruncher is this year's good-for-nothing PCjr. Upgrades are necessary at least once a year to keep your PC, at the very least, usable and, at most, in fashion.

In order to make the upgrade process safer for both you and your computer, here are tips on how to prepare for a PC upgrade:

- To ensure that you have the physical stamina to last through the upgrade, start working out aerobically at least four to five weeks in advance. Three weeks prior to the upgrade, start lifting weights twice daily. A week before the upgrade, bulk up on carbohydrates and Gatorade.

- Ask your spouse and children to leave the house before you start the upgrade. Tell your children that when they return to the house you may not look like the same person. You will probably be sweat-stained, disheveled, with ragged clothes and wild hair. You'll have dark rings around your eyes. You'll probably smell pretty bad too. And you won't act the same either. You'll be irritable. Little things will scare you, like the "ping-ping" of the refrigerator's ice-cube maker. You'll sleep for days at a time. You may wake up screaming in the night. The dog will avoid you. But tell the children not to worry, because eventually you'll return to normal, maybe even in as little as two to three months.

- Give your spouse specific instructions about what to do if they don't hear from you in four or five weeks. Tell them that UNDER NO CIRCUM-STANCES ARE THEY TO GO NEAR THE HOUSE. Instead they should call 911. If they see rescue workers lead you from the house disoriented, they are to IMMEDIATELY head to an automated teller. They should withdraw all money from any joint checking and savings accounts. Then they are to hurry back to the house, cancel all credit cards, and destroy any computer parts and repair catalogs with 800 numbers that might be lying around. This is to make sure you don't blow the family's savings on computer parts to try to fix what you broke during the upgrade.

- Wear loose-fitting clothing that you do not care about, just in case it gets soiled or burned—or ripped apart in an emergency room.

- Stock your own emergency medical chest near the computer. Include aspirin, compresses, fingertip bandages, Pepto-Bismol, Mercurochrome, and nine to ten bottles of really cheap vodka. Also include emergency supplies like candles and granola bars in case the electricity goes out in the house for more than three days.

- Remove all weapons from the room where the PC resides. This includes baseball bats, scissors, squirt guns, knitting needles, letter openers, flower pots, clarinets, large phone books, and anything else you might use to harm the PC in a moment of insane irritation.

- Remember that if you can't get the PC working again after the upgrade, it will make a really special gift for those out-of-town in-laws who've always wanted a PC. Just make sure you change your phone number after you give it to them.

How to Make Friends on the
Information Highway

Information Highway Tip #82b

L og on with the name "Buffy." Ask a really dumb technical question. When you respond to the replies, allude
to the fact that you're 24 years old, the spitting image of the
model on the cover of that month's Victoria's Secret catalog,
extremely athletic, employed in a managerial position at Microsoft, and like to use your computer naked.

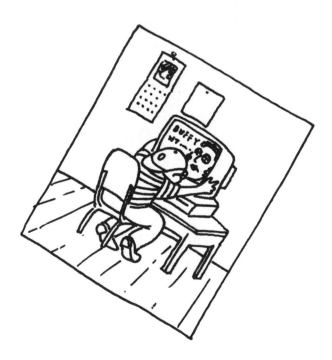

What to Do the Morning After You've Spilled Your Guts in an E-mail Message to 80 Million People Around the World

The Information Highway induces intimate confessions with the ease of a Geraldo. One minute you're innocently typing a message about the odd sounds coming from your disk drive. The next you've removed the wax from the jelly glass of your soul and dumped out the emotional goo, from details of your loveless childhood to sordid tales of the aliens who begot you. With the flick of a key, you impulsively shoot that E-mail message into cyberspace to be planted on 80 million computers from Iowa City to Baghdad. The next morning you awaken with a sense of foreboding. You have just invited millions of weird strangers who go by names like snotface@cyber.edu into the private Holocaust of your soul. What to do?

Obviously, the last thing you want to do is log on to a computer. But you must. You need to begin damage control. It's not that these weird characters will make fun of you. Oh, no, it's much worse than that. Rather, they will flood you with E-mail messages detailing their own personal problems. Within hours, you'll have so many E-mail messages chronicling other people's problems that you'll feel like Dear Abby during the Christmas rush.

The easiest thing to do would be to say that someone broke into your office in the middle of the night, stole your computer password, and wrote a fake message with your name on it. But no one would believe that. That's like saying your dog ate your math homework. Everybody on the info-highway uses it to weasel out of things. What you need is an E-mail form letter that you can mail out to those thousands of people who will try to sympathize with you. Here's one to get you started:

Dear Cyber Friend,

It is good to know that people like you sympathize with my problems. I have a lot of problems. But so do you, as I can see from your E-mail message. In fact, I was really impressed with the number of intra-personal/job-related/marriage-related/incarceration-related (circle one)

problems that you have. They make mine seem not so bad. In fact, I feel pretty good now. That is one of the neat things about the info-highway: we all have problems and we can send each other messages about them. Boy, this technology stuff is great!

Thank you for your E-mail message. I can't tell you the profound difference it made in my life. Thanks to you I am now convinced that I am normal/in need of a therapist/a victim of an alien abduction/not dying of a weird disease/a child of an illegal union in talk.bizarre (circle one).

You will always remain My Special Cyber Friend.

Cordially,

Joe

By the Light of the Cathode Moon: Information Highway Love Tips

Has your sweet patootie jumped ship? Has your love conquest of the night disappeared forever in a public restroom? Fret not. Armed with but a personal computer and a wrist corsage, you too can play Casanova on the Information Highway. Guaranteed!

T he days when it was easy to wow dates with massive stereo systems and rhinestone cowboy boots may be long past, but that's no cause for despair. The art of deploying high-tech toys in wooing Information Highway babes and beefcakes is in its infancy. The rules of wooing by personal computer are simple: keep the relationship software-based until you run out of champagne, and if the hard disk crashes before the evening's over, salvage the evening with a couple TV dinners and an Intel sales motivation tape played on the VCR. Beyond that, everything else is a matter of personal style.

In the hope of helping you, dearest friend, to refine that personal amoroso style, the following Information Highway love tips have been culled from a variety of authoritative (although mostly anonymous) sources. Like plumbing conventions in May, home computers are indeed aphrodisiacal. Don't let any sex-starved Luddite convince you otherwise.

When Eros Makes Use of Plastic Tablecloths

Here's how to do it. Before your lucky love-duck appears at the door, tidy up the PC and the area around it. You'll want to give your ardent amorist the impression that you are one of the most potent of Information Age caballeros, a computer power user.

To this end, hide or remove all evidence that you have at any point in your life hit, kicked, punched, bitten, or otherwise mutilated your PC in frustration. Should the machine display dents, fingernail scratches, or tooth marks from such attacks, camouflage them with rhododendrons or air ferns. If the PC looks like a victim in a relationship gone awry, cover it completely with a large plastic tablecloth. Scorch marks around wall outlets, suggesting electronic reprisals of the past, should be masked by an application of redwood picnic table stain.

In His or Her Mind, You Should
Always Be a Power User

Next, remove from the wall any maps of brightly colored rug yarn that depict where your spelling checker's subdirectory is located in relation to your desk chair. Some champagne brunch companions find these a turn-off. Remove from the PC any Post-It notes that advise "This is where the floppy disk goes" or "Insert expanded memory card here." Hide all CDs that teach structured programming through the singing of *Sesame Street* songs. Stash any paperback computer books with "Intended for K-1 through K-4" printed on the back. The last thing you want is for your bawdy buttercup to discover that all those clever witticisms you've been muttering all night about MOS transistors were plagiarized from Winnie & Winthrup's *First Computer: Finding Out About Binary.*

Tell Her, Yes Tell Her What
"Programmable Logic" Means!

Lest you consider the job done, be advised that it has merely begun. Charm is as much a matter of having the right software utilities as it is getting the WD-40 properly chilled in the backup tape vault. As any online Lothario can tell you, you can never have too many disk utilities that transform all your executables into sweet nothings, your object modules into Lionel Richie song lyrics, and your screen cursor into a winking heart.

Be sure to keep on hand lots of software that beeps. Like chocolate, the heart in love never tires of software that beeps. Other date pleasers include full-screen program source code debuggers that make splashing waterfall sounds, text editors that work with an incense burner, object-oriented operating systems in which all the objects are anatomically correct, and fortune-telling software that makes loud, grinding disk reading sounds as it searches out the star signs.

Choreograph all your keyboard moves in advance. Be sure to include enough hard disk directory sorts to keep your love puppy entranced. Plan to explain the phrase "office computer network" at least twice. Demonstrate to your cupid kitten how massive amounts of computer data regularly scroll their way across your computer's screen and, amazingly, never seem to get lost. Scatter heart-shaped pillows liberally around the analog test equipment.

When His Eyes Are as Witchy
as DOS in the Dark

What now? you ask. How does one proceed from heart-shaped pillows to dynamic data exchange? How does one motor to the drive-in when the keyboard cable won't reach that far?

If you are a bus-cruising bon vivant you already know the answer: you take out your copy of *Point and Shoot Without a Cause* and gun the motherboard toward the moon. All down the road, with the wind singing through your transistors, you pat your dainty datakin's optical mouse, press the <Number-Lock> key all the way to the floor, and rhapsodize about what it means to be a rebel in a classic bus without a speed-up crystal. Eventually you stop for malts.

And should your goo-goo kitten ask for copies of your hard disk crash diagnostic software, you'll know that you are finally experiencing high-bit romance on the Information Highway.

The PC Turns into a
"This Space for Sale" Sign

Stupid PC Trick #482

A ctually, this is not such a bad thing to have happen.
Many computer professionals earn extra $$ by renting
out their office PC's screen to billboard advertisers.
Whenever the PC is idle or something malfunc-
tions, the screen turns itself into a gaudy four-
color poster for Pete's Electrolysis or
Windy City Office Repair, and the PC
owners earn extra cash during their ma-
chine's down time.

If you own an IBM PC compatible
and run Microsoft Windows, here's how
you can turn your PC into a "This Space
for Sale" sign:

1. Head to Windows' Program
    Manager. Click on the main icon.

2. In the Main window, click on the con-
    trol panel icon. Now click on desktop.

3. In the Screen Saver box, under name, choose
    marquee.

4. Click setup.

5. Choose a background color for the sign by clicking on the down arrow, then clicking on the color that you want.

6. In the Text box, type this space for rent

7. Click on format text.

8. Choose a font by clicking on the font name. Under Font Style, click on Bold. Under size, click on 72.

9. To choose a color for the letters, click on the down arrow and click on the color.

Now click OK. Click your way back through the windows by clicking on OK in each window.

How to Obtain Psychiatric Advice on the Information Highway

Information Highway Tip #14

A s many millions of people are discovering, the Information Highway is a great place to seek free psychiatric advice. This is because so many of its users have already spent so much time in counseling—and also have enough free time on their hands to send total strangers thousands of E-mail messages about what they've learned.

For your advice, start by typing all your problems, personal as well as professional, into one long E-mail message. Do not include paragraph indents or bother to write in sentences. The more rambling the message appears, the better. If you can include a Kilroy character fashioned out of keyboard signs, all the better.

Now log onto the freewheeling worldwide computer network Internet. Copy your message into all five thousand public message groups. Send multiple copies to the message group called talk.bizarre and to any message groups that sound like they have something to do with international problems, UFOs, Rush Limbaugh, or cats. Now log off. Wait 24 hours, then log back on.

You'll probably find about 50,000 E-mail messages waiting for you. Erase all the ones from people with dumb-sounding logons like reckless.sin and con.dum. Also erase all the ones in which correspondents don't offer any advice on your problems but merely detail their own (you'll be able to spot these messages by the fact that they'll be the longest). This will leave about ninety messages.

Now erase all the messages from people who profess to "use the Net to explore alternative facets of [their] personality." Erase all the ones that appear to be from fringe Freudian analysts who perform bizarre experiments on ski jumps with carbon monoxide and Bazooka bubble gum. Erase all the ones from Jungian analysts fixated upon finding the archetypes in the old TV show *Family Ties*. Erase all the ones advising that you cover yourself in peanut butter and play Jane Fonda workout videos backwards all day, looking for hidden clues about space alien abductions. If you're lucky, you will probably have one or two pithy messages remaining. Chances are they will cut through the psychobabble and tell you exactly what to do. In all likelihood that advice will be: "Getalife!"

Shop Till You Disconnect

True Info-Highway Adventure!

Taking Advantage of Good Buys on
the Information Highway

I live in a neighborhood with a lot of mini-malls, but I prefer to do as much shopping as I can via modem—and all the major mail retailers now hawk products through computer services, including J.C. Penney, Spiegel, Sears, Brooks Brothers, and Lands' End. There is nothing like the thrill you get when you receive in the mail something you ordered based on a fuzzy picture on a computer screen.

Take the waterbed sheets, for example. I must have tapped my way around a dozen commercial online services looking for waterbed sheets in a delft pattern with coyotes stamped around the edges. I finally found them in a little-known designer sheets catalog outlet on Internet. The picture that I downloaded looked like an armload of radiation-treated fabric piled in a hospital laundry hamper, but I knew through past online shopping experiences that the picture bore little relation to what would eventually arrive in the mail. Thankfully it did not. The sheets glowed even more than the ones I saw online.

The amazing thing about these online stores is that they have precisely tailored their sales pitches to appeal to the computer-geek psyche. For instance, I have no need to see what my clothes look like before I buy them. Nor do I have any need to try them on. The J.C. Penney store on Prodigy knows this. Rather than provide grainy computer graphics of apparel, they stick to bland descriptions. "After a long day of work," reads one, "you will look forward to slipping on this cable-knit pullover. Styled with the casual look you love to relax in."

Clothing retailers tend to offer a lot of underwear for sale online. In fact, Spiegel's entire women's clothing line on Prodigy consists of stretch velvet bras and boxer shorts. While I admit these are the staples of my own wardrobe—and I do have days at the computer when this is all I wear—I have occasionally yearned for an "Egyptian Fresco Necktie" like the one sold by the Metropolitan Museum of Art on CompuServe. Its computer picture looks like the tongue of a grizzly bear that has just swallowed hot milk.

Household furnishings is where the online service stores shine. If you're like me, you would prefer not to have to look at furniture and drapes before you buy them. You like to be surprised. The Basset Furniture computer picture showroom on CompuServe will paint its "Arts & Crafts Dining Room" on your screen. It is a greenish room that looks like it has just been invaded by a poltergeist from the movie of the same name. On the positive side, the furniture does look neatly arranged.

The Metropolitan Museum of Art offers a large variety of art prints on CompuServe, including Alexandre Cabanel's *The Birth of Venus*. It is indistinguishable from the "Arts & Crafts Dining Room."

My favorite thing to shop for online is flowers. 800-Flowers on CompuServe sells an attractive bouquet called a "Tropical Arrangement." Unfortunately, its computer picture is a bit deceiving. It looks like a fire-breathing dragon is attacking the anthuriums, and a naked man is fleeing into a cave behind the protea. The real arrangement is nowhere near as scintillating. The "P.G.A. Golf Basket" similarly suffers in translation. Its digital drawing makes it look like a gluey blob of Jell-O with a golf ball planted in the middle.

There are ads for General Motor's Saturn cars all over Prodigy. I tried to order one online, but unfortunately General Motors insisted on having a local dealer call me. I did not like that at all. I do not like to talk to people I prefer sales situations in which I can just tap my credit card number into a computer and something will arrive in the mail in a few days. I would like to order a Saturn that way. I don't care about the color, or the number of bucket seats. I just want to pick it out from a cartoonish sketch on Prodigy and have it arrive in the mail. Are you listening, General Motors? They probably think that, being a computer geek, my major retail purchase for the year will be waterbed sheets that glow. They might just be right.

Business Card E-mail Advice

Information Highway Tip #76

Having an E-mail address on your business card is the ultimate '90s status symbol. It tells the world that you're with it, info-highway-wise, and hobnob with Al Gore on Internet.

Here are a few tips:

- Print your E-mail address at the very bottom of the card below your street address, as if to say, "Who receives snail-mail anymore?" But don't make it any bigger than your street address, or people might confuse you with a real geek.

- Make sure that your E-mail address sounds as juvenile as possible. A good example is pigface@ prodigy.com or french-fry-snorter@aol.com.

- List more than one E-mail address, three if you're in a high-tech field. At least one of the E-mail addresses should be an Internet address. (Internet addresses have an @ sign in the middle that people who are not in the know, information-highway-wise, call "that 'a' thing.")

- Print the entire address in lowercase letters to ensure that your messages travel on all international
  E-mail systems without any hassle. Another info
  status requirement to be sure.

- If you work at a university, make your E-mail
  address look as imposing and hieroglyphic as possible. That is the only way to be taken seriously at a
  university. For example:

  frank@uucp.cosi!fan!tutte!bitnet!down!with!the!
  middle!class@berkeley.edu

- Avoid numbers because you don't want your E-mail
  address to be mistaken for a retail store price register code.

My Business Partner Attacks
the Customer Database

Horrifying True Stories from the Technological Jungle

I f you ever want to go into business with someone, you should choose a partner who is hardworking, reliable, and smart. You should also find one who tackles problems in creative ways.

My business partner—let's call him Frank—is all of these things. He is one of the hardest working people I know, and one of the smartest too. When it comes to crafty assaults on tricky problems, Frank can best most captains of industry. But every once in a while, when we least expect it, something in him short-circuits. A fuse blows, the lights flicker, and suddenly we are plummeting into chaos.

This is what happened recently when Frank collided with the customer database.

Frank and I publish a newsletter. It is devoted to using the Information Highway to research investments, and hence make lots of money—a feat that we have yet to accomplish, but it doesn't mean our readers can't. It is a modest undertaking, but we give it all our heart. We both maintain offices on opposite ends of the country, thanks to the miracle of faxes and electronic mail—neither of which we are very good at getting to work in a consistent manner.

We had just done a glitzy mass mailing, and new subscriptions were rolling in faster than soap suds over the top of an overloaded washing machine.

Frank exuberantly set about processing orders. I offered to help, but Frank said, "No, no, you have more important things to do. Let me handle it."

I frowned when he said this. All those orders—thousands of them—had to be keyed into the customer database. I knew Frank wasn't a good typist but he was resourceful. I figured he'd either hire a temp, turn the orders over to an order-processing firm, or give his mom $25 bucks to key them in for him.

When I didn't hear from him for a week, I started to worry. I called him, but when he answered the phone, he just grunted and said, "These orders are taking me a lot longer to process than I thought."

Another week passed. I called again. "I'm still typing," Frank replied laconically.

But by the third week, Frank had finished processing the orders. He was understandably jubilant about it. "The money's in the bank," he declared, "the printer's bills are paid, and I'm cranking out the next issue. Things are really rolling here." I congratulated him. I told him that, for a spell there, I actually worried about whether he'd be able to cope with all that clerical work.

"Well," he hemmed. "There is one problem." The long distance phone line fell into silence. "You see..." He cleared his throat. His voice dropped the way it does whenever the Hand of Judgment is about to pass over our small venture and possibly stop and slap it about, knock it dizzy. My hands clenched in tension.

"When I started processing the orders," Frank began, "I separated the checks and the envelopes from the order blanks. I put the checks in one pile on my desk, you see, and I put the envelopes in another pile on my desk, and then I put the credit card numbers in a third pile, and as I started keying names and addresses into the subscriber database, I kept referring to these piles, and I tried to keep things straight, but—" He cleared his throat again. "By the time I was done," he chuckled nervously, "I ended up with a lot more names in the customer database than I did checks and credit card numbers."

"How many more?" I asked.

He stopped chuckling. "Hundreds."

Frank then told me what he had done. He sent all the new customers a letter explaining the situation. It went something like this:

Dear Friend,

Your name is in our customer database. Unfortunately, I can't figure out why. Maybe you ordered a subscription. Maybe you sent us a check or your credit card number. If so, we'd like to thank you and assure you that your subscription will be in the mail just as soon as you tell us if this is what you did. Maybe you did not send us any money. If so, please tell us if this is what you did, and if so, what you want.

Please reply ASAP by return mail.

I promise you this mix-up will never happen again.

Thanks,

Frank
Publisher and CEO

After Frank divulged the contents of his letter, I gasped, "You didn't!"

"What other choice did I have?" he said.

"How many customers did you send it to?"

"All of them."

I groaned.

The one bright spot in this whole fiasco is that if we lost any customers, there is no way we will ever know.

Frank was apologetic about the screw-up, philosophical even. "At least we now have a clearer understanding of why people have so many problems getting their magazine subscriptions," he said.

Now you see why we have yet to make any money on the Information Highway. But don't let that stop you. Maybe we've just taken the wrong approach.

Your PC Makes Everyone
in the World Think That
Professional People Don't Cry

Stupid PC Trick #17

T he biggest problem with PCs is that you can't tell anyone that your PC made you cry. Being a computer
magazine advice columnist, I get letters all the time from
successful professionals who, in the course of trying to do
something simple like print a spreadsheet, have been reduced to blubbering mounds of human wreckage, the floors
around their desks littered by wads of Kleenex. They can't
tell their co-workers, they can't tell their bosses for fear of
having "hit and run victim on info-highway" scribbled ominously in their personnel folders for the
rest of their working lives. They can't tell their
families either, and they certainly can't go
on *Oprah* and talk about it. It is the
greatest stigma in our society today: re-
vealing that you can't boot up your PC
without being reduced to tears. The
amazing thing is, as computers become
simpler to use, the number of people
they have reduced to tears grows expo-
nentially larger. One can only hope
that one day computers will become so simple to use that the number of tearful sufferers will become so great
that employer will no longer make fun of them.

"Proposal for New National Holiday Relevant to U.S. as Leader of High Technology"

From the *Congressional Record*

HON. BORIS Q. POPINRATH of Arkansas
in the House of Representatives

Mr. POPINRATH. Mr. Speaker, as you know, our nation is struggling to remain the world leader in high technology. Overseas chip fabrication is booming, while it is becoming increasingly difficult to buy big chip cookies in bulk in my home state. The Japanese have already seized the high ground in high-resolution television, while many of the people in my home state still have small black-and-white sets. To hear *Time* magazine tell it, superconductivity cars are the wave of the future, but there are presently no superconductivity cars in the State of Arkansas. Not a one. This can only lead one to conclude that they are all overseas.

This is a dire state of affairs, Mr. Speaker, as you can see, and we in the Land of Opportunity State would like to do something about it. To this end, I and a committee of ladies have decided that the best place to start in restoring the United States' reputation as a leader of worldwide technology would be to honor the many casualties of workplace automation here in the State of Arkansas. To fund these efforts we could sell small items like toaster covers with the official state mineral stenciled on them. The proceeds would be used to buy grave markers to commemorate the resting places of the *e populus* uni foot soldiers of technology: the public workers who have died learning to use their computers. We estimate that this will keep us busy until the next election.

We also believe it would boost morale considerably among state office workers if Congress were to establish a new national holiday honoring government employees who have died learning to use their computers. It could be something along the lines of the new National Seasonal Temperature Range Statistics Day. We believe it would boost government employee morale even more if this new holiday were positioned conveniently between Joey Stoppelmoore, Philanthropist of the Past Day and Poultry Processing Secession Day on a sunny weekend in June, when state office workers would be more favorably inclined to spend the day in recreative contemplation of the demise of their co-workers than on a cold, gloomy one.

My office would be more than happy to publicize this new holiday. The ladies' committee, which has recently adopted the name The Daughters of the American Robotron Revolution, is already enthusiastically organizing the sale of all necessary toaster covers.

As a people, as a well-meaning society, as Americans, we have a responsibility to remember those dauntless government workers who so bravely gave their lives in the course of learning how to use their computers. Our country's founders would have. Joey Stoppelmoore would have. As you can see, much is happening in the Regnat Populus State. Much that we can all learn a lesson from.

Arkansas is proud to be leading the way in the crusade to bring chip-making back to the United States. The simple act of declaring a federal holiday for our nation to remember its many Arkansan computer victims may not in itself bring chip-tilling back to our shores, but it is a fine start for any session of Congress.

Mr. Speaker, my fine colleagues, I ask you to join with me in supporting the new Arkansas Public Workers Who Have Died Learning to Use Their Computers Somber Memorial and Picnic Commemorative Day. It just may mean the difference between our nation's being taken seriously as a world technology leader and being laughed at ignominiously by the likes of the Japanese.

The PC Pretends It's a Border Collie and Ends Up at the City Pound

Stupid PC Trick #8210

This problem is more common than most PC owners suspect. One day your PC is sitting primly on your desk, inexhaustibly calculating the cells of your spreadsheet. Suddenly, it disappears. A few days later you find it at the pound, cowering behind the chain-links of a kennel, between a psychotic ex-police dog and a delusional basset hound.

You go to the front desk and complain, but the attendant can only sputter, "But we were sure it was a border collie! We found it sitting in the middle of Highway G with a rubber ball in its mouth. It came when we called 'Lucky'!"

The problems don't stop there either. When you take the PC back to your office, you discover that, not only does it stink for weeks like a wet dog, but the only thing it will accept in its CD-ROM drive is rawhide chew chips. Whenever you type DIR for a hard disk directory, the drive spins with the growl of a junkyard dog and keeps reminiscing to you about its appearance on late-night television news as "Pet of the Week."

The only solution? Let the cat sit on the keyboard.

Desire Among the Binary Trees

A True Information Highway Romance!

The breeze bobbling in the memory interleaves, the scent of magnolia in the ASCII data streams, these are the things that make love bloom in the Kingdom of Binary. Through the miracle of frequency modulated billets-doux, Bitsy Batchfile and Captain BIOS discover that love is half Boolean, half delusion.

H e called her "Bitsy Batchfile," she called him "Captain BIOS." They met in a message thread on EEPROM blasting on a computer bulletin board in Pocatello, Idaho. From the first it was like Eros-muxed phase jitter in a multi-drop infatuation. He was smitten with her knowledge of interrupt handlers, she with his video ROM. Before they knew it they were swapping DOS calls at high speed over packet-switched lines.

Captain BIOS had led a wildcard life. Between his fondness for female connectors and Boolean algebra, he had frittered away his youthful up-time until his coprocessors were hoary, his checksums shot. Ensconced now in a house-trailer in a double-density bayou, he liked to reminisce fondly about the pioneer days of floating-point processors. He polished his old Winchesters. Sometimes he drank too much and had a problem with fragmented files.

Bitsy Batchfile was a delicate VAXen with laugh wrinkles around her command prompt. Her husband had left her for a dot-matrix printer with an injection-molded travel case, then later shot himself in a Nevada motel room when he discovered that no one made ribbons for it any longer. Her manner was soft-sectored. Her software library was as wildly eclectic as the contents of a system analyst's pockets.

Each night, Captain BIOS would leave Bitsy tender machine instructions in her electronic mailbox. She'd respond with coy conditionals, telling him of hibiscus that bloomed in the pin-outs of her soul, of her love of small children and analog signals, of how she thought of him at night when parity breezes blew through the sybaritic data structures of her windowed environment.

Devotedly, Captain BIOS would spool her messages into discrete data files for later off-line printing. Bitsy did likewise with his. The computer bulletin board became a lovers' nest, a nightly rendezvous spot with twinkling data set ready lights, and Bitsy and the Captain became the Tristan and Isolde of trellis-encoded hearts and flowers. The fact that they had never swapped parity bits in person only further electrified the ardency of their long-distanced error-checked desire. As far as each could see, the other was nothing less than a perfectly schematized Lothario or Dulcinea with shapely Erlang measurements and a complete set of programming tools. Far be it for anything in the stars or stop bits to suggest otherwise.

It was only after both had racked up long-distance phone bills big enough to fuel the bailout of a bankrupt long-distance carrier that both agreed to an in-person hexadecimal dump.

The day arrived when both found themselves sauntering through the cocktail lounge of Denver's Stapleton Airport. It was a point halfway between the computers of both. At the preclocked time, in the preprogrammed way, both took seats on opposite sides of the piano bar and ordered raspberry cremes.

Over his raspberry creme, Captain BIOS ogled Bitsy. He fretted that she had failed to tell him about her double-chin file allocation table.

Over her raspberry creme, Bitsy snuck a peek at BIOS. She despaired that he had conveniently failed to mention the generous design specifications of his middle-aged memory maps.

BIOS sipped more of his drink and, with snotty disgust, concluded that Bitsy wore dark stockings to conceal her VAXicose veins.

Bitsy plunged her spoon into her drink, smirkily noting that BIOS needed at least two bar stools to hold up his backplane.

BIOS concluded that Bitsy's hair was hopelessly full of static.

Bitsy concluded that she would never find true floating-point happiness with a male coprocessor who looked so obviously like a lush.

Eventually, Bitsy Batchfile and Captain BIOS moved their bar stools to the same side of the piano bar, if only to appear polite.

Upon discovering, though, to the surprise of neither, that neither had much to say to the other beyond the pleasant exchange of dBASE version numbers, both got back on their respective planes and flew all the way back across the country to their respective computers.

Once home, both breathed a sigh of relief that the ordeal was over.

Captain BIOS and Bitsy Batchfile still hang out in the EEPROM-blasting message thread on the computer bulletin board in Pocatello, Idaho, but their exchanges have cooled. Bitsy has since directed numerous cross-compiling innuendoes toward a hulking random number generator by the name of Isochronous Thor. Captain BIOS, meanwhile, has been feverishly trying to captivate a gaggle of giggling quicksort groupies.

(In the minds of both, it is all for the best, for neither was ready to cash in their chips for anything less than true binary love.)

Your PC Overdosed on Your Son's Orange Soda and Now It Won't Work

Stupid PC Trick #31

This is another of the oldest PC tricks in the book. One minute your 11-year-old is happily playing Doom. The next minute he's screaming, "Mom! The PC stopped working!" You investigate. You find the keyboard swimming in orange soda.

What happened is one of those gut-wrenching occurrences that reveal the dark nature of computers. The PC literally wrenched the soda can from your son's hand. It guzzled itself witless, then, when it had too much, it burped up the excess all over the keyboard.

The amazing thing is, PCs only do this in the presence of small boys—small boys who are rarely believed when they recount incredible tales of the treacheries of the world around them. Invariably, you won't believe your son when he tells you what the PC did. You'll blame it on him. You'll tell him it's a figment of his imagination, that he's making up stories after he spilled soda on the keyboard. That's what the PC wants you to do. Now you know how smart PCs really are.

You'll Meet All Kinds of People on the Information Highway

W hen you log on to the Information Highway you'll meet all sorts of powerful, well-connected people like yourself. That's not surprising because powerful, well-connected people often have lots of time on their hands, and what better way to spend it than to call a former Defense Department network and write dozens of E-mail messages about whether you identify more with the Sean Connery "James Bond" or the Roger Moore one? Here are just a few of the well-connected people you'll meet if you hang out long enough on the Information Highway.

EVER TALKED TO GUYS WHO EAT REAL GREASY FOOD AND NEED A DATE?

YOU WILL

Dale Ozolitis, also known as "oleo@maximum. com": The star pupil of the Arizona maximum security prison computer lab, Dale is known for the witty, erudite quotes in his E-mail signatures. In Internet's talk.bizarre conference he is admired for his almost encyclopedic knowledge of *Lost in Space* episodes. For his E-mail pen pals, this is proof enough that he is what he says he is: president of a

Fortune 500 company with an abiding interest in chickens. Many in this conference also rely on Dale for expert advice on buying long-term bonds, protecting their cars with anti-theft devices, and whether or not to clone their spouses (a frequent topic of conversation). But little do the innocents in talk.bizarre know that Dale is renowned throughout the penal system of the western half of the United States for 478 prison escape attempts, all of which entailed spray-painting his body silver in the hope that he could pass in front of prison security cameras undetected.

Heather, also known as "lady.venus@love.com": Poor Heather, she's in love with oleo@maximum.com, not just because he's a multimillionaire like he says he is, but because of his vast and profound knowledge of *Lost in Space* episodes. To think she wasted almost a decade of her life posting thousands of E-mail messages a week about *Star Trek* when she would have found true love faster had she posted messages about *Lost in Space* instead. (The problem with the *Star Trek* conferences is that there's just not enough room to type into them all of one's emotional problems. While there is in talk.bizarre.) It's a good thing that oleo@maximum.com is a multimillionaire, because he can help her pay for her therapy. The bill is sure to be quite high ever since her brother tried to get her to watch every single *Cheers* episode. She did, but without laughing once.

Detective Henry, also known as "cyber-cop@police. org": He is actually Al, an undercover police officer searching for embezzlers, con artists, thieves, and other low-lifes on the Information Highway. Al wants to be detective someday, and that's why he goes by the nom de plume "Detective Henry." He had originally planned to masquerade as the president of a Fortune 500 company with an abiding interest in chickens, but he noticed that there was already such a company president in talk.bizarre. He spends most of his time these days in talk.bizarre. He keeps the door to his office at the precinct shut, as he intently reads the messages in talk.bizarre, and when other officers knock on it, he grumps, "Go away! I'm busy slapping some sense into a witness!" All the other officers admire Al for his dedication to the administration of justice. As for Al, he cannot figure out why, after he joked in a message he wrote in talk.bizarre that one could pass undetected in front of police security cameras by spray-painting one's body silver, hundreds of attempted prison breaks were staged around the country by inmates trying this technique.

Louis, also known as "deranged@univ.edu": Louis is as dangerous as they come on the Information Highway. He is a university administrator with too much time on his hands. Hour after hour he types in scrupulous messages about curriculum models, university football teams, the diseases of his co-workers, and his favorite dairy bars on campus. Louis's university makes the mistake of rating his job performance by how many E-mail messages he answers in a day. Louis's performance has been soaring ever since he stumbled on talk.bizarre. He has met many delightful people there, like the Fortune 500 president who knows all about car alarms (he advised Louis on fixing his own), or the little boy who wants to grow up to be a police detective. He has even learned about spray-painting his body silver so that he doesn't set off his office's security monitor when he works late at night. Talk.bizarre has certainly enriched his life. He even invested all his retirement money in the company called X-Industries that everyone there talks so fondly about. When he sent the money, in unmarked bills, to the Fortune 500 CEO, he never got a receipt, but that hardly troubles him. He knows you can trust the strangers you meet on the Information Highway more than you can trust your own children.

Your PC Makes You Think That
It Can Save You Time

Stupid PC Trick #1903

This is one of the oldest tricks in the book. PCs are too complicated to ever be truly useful. There is nothing that a PC can do in a day that one slow-moving, easily confused $4.50-an-hour temporary office worker can't do in thirty minutes. As a PC demands more time to complete a task, a human being will require less time. Even a $4.50-an-hour human being. That is one of the secret laws of computer science: computers are faster than people but only when people are brain-dead.

The funny thing is, most consumers realize this immediately upon opening up the boxes of their new computer, but they forget it after they've owned a PC for a few months. As soon as they accomplish some trivial task with the computer, despite weeks of Herculean struggle, they let their guard down and start smiling at the computer. In reality, this is when they should start to worry.

It won't be long before the PC tricks them into thinking that they actually enjoy squinting at a TV screen so blurry it would make an air traffic controller crazy, or that they look forward to sifting through obtuse, phone-book size computer manuals that make IRS publications look like beach reading.

The reality is that PCs were not made to help you get things done. They were made to sell a bizillion machines and make rich men of skinny guys in mad-scientist glasses. They were designed to spawn a whole industry that would employ dweeby guys with calculators on their belts who couldn't get jobs refilling vending machines.

Don't let the PC's aura of efficiency make you forget that if you didn't have it you would have room for both a philodendron and a ceramic cat on your desk.

Office Tower Collapses Under Weight of Digital Information Glut

From *U.S. Scoop* & *Scandal Today*

NEW YORK—Popular misgivings about the Information Age were bolstered today when a large office building in downtown Manhattan collapsed under the weight of a digital information surplus. Insiders say that workers in the building had misgivings about the tonnage of raw computer data being stored in the tower. Their concern began as early as two years ago when a large accounting firm inhabiting the top floors began amassing unusually large computer databases.

According to reports, employees of the accounting firm claimed that the equivalent of 800,000 sets of *Encyclopedia Britannica* flowed into the offices hourly over electronic data lines. Some started to worry that the firm had created more computer databases in their offices than could safely be supported by the building's steel frame.

Rescue workers are still combing the wreckage for survivors. Everyone who was inside the building at the time of the collapse has been accounted for—miraculously, there were no injuries—but world-weary rescue workers remain skeptical. They point to the mastodonic databases found amid the debris. "Getting hit by one of those would be like getting beaned by Mount Rushmore," said one. Cranes are being brought in to remove the boulder-like information caches before they drop through the earth to sewers and subways below.

The disaster hit early this morning. A maintenance worker inside the building heard what sounded like creaking timbers coming from a computer room in the accounting firm's sprawling offices. Recalling that the firm had a reputation for collecting dangerously large amounts of data with little or no regard to its density, the workers fled.

Within minutes, the 82-story concrete and glass tower was reduced to dusty rubble. The maintenance worker was later quoted as saying, "I always knew computer databases were heavy, but doesn't this beat all?"

Experts say that this tragedy is just the start of what will probably grow into a worldwide epidemic in the coming years. As databases grow bigger, we'll see more office buildings crack and crumble under the weight. According to structural engineer T.Y. Bin (who asked to remain nameless), "Modern architecture is simply not prepared to handle the deluge of electronic data that will flood into the workplace of tomorrow. You have to remember, we are limited to building with steel and concrete. We have yet to invent a substance strong enough to support the weight of almost limitless knowledge."

Until then, he and others warn that more office tower collapses like the one today in Manhattan are an inevitable consequence of the Information Age. "This is the price we pay for putting everything into machine readable form," said another structural engineer, Abolhassan Bastaneh.

How to Turn Your PC into
Seymour's Plant

Stupid PC Trick #1001

Y ou can make your PC more like Seymour's plant in Little Shop of Horrors by adding a few lines to your autoexec.bat file. (This file contains the instructions the PC reads and follows when you turn it on.) Just follow these simple steps:

1. In your word processor, load the file C:\autoexec.bat. The autoexec.bat on your PC may be stored on a hard drive other than the C: one. If so, use that drive letter when you load the file.

2. At the very end of the autoexec.bat file add the lines

    @echo off

    echo FEED ME!!!!

    pause

3. You don't want to save the file with word processor formatting, so select the word processor option to save it as "text with carriage returns" or "ASCII." Be sure to save the file to the root

directory of your hard disk—the place where it was stored originally.

4. Reboot the computer by pressing the reset button on the front or pressing the <alt><ctrl><del> keys all at once. Now stand back.

Glossary

O n the Information Highway the shape of technological innovation changes daily. The spelling does too. For the edification of aspiring cyberpunks as well as old console hands, the following lexicon has been provided. With this glossary in hand, we hope that you'll never again find yourself asking sheepishly "Which way to my E-mail address?"

Autoexec.bat File Separates gutless computer wimps from the masters of the universe. Masters of the universe have huge autoexec.bat files containing a florid number of ECHO OFF commands, gratuitous GOSUBs, and quotes from Gandhi. Gutless computer wimps have four-line autoexec.bat files that actually work.

Big Information Database (BID) A collection of mostly irrelevant information that you will never use. *See* Information.

Box (BX)   What a computer comes in. Its size is only sur-
passed by the number of promises printed on the box of
things that the computer will never actually do.

Brave New World   Something you get when you mail off
cereal box tops to Bill Nye Science Guy on PBS.

Cable (CBL)   What hangs off the back of your PC. If
there's only one of them, you forgot the other six in the
trunk of your car.

Clinton, President Bill   Only world leader who is almost
as powerful as Bill Gates. (*See* Gates, Bill.) Also, first U.S.
president with an E-mail box. Unfortunately, some of his E-
mail comes to me—especially the mail from a particularly
disgruntled constituent named Harry on CompuServe. *See*
Harry on CompuServe.

Computer   Secret weapon designed by alien race in con-
junction with now defunct communist government to slow
capitalism to a halt by preventing anyone from getting any
work done. Extremely effective.

Computer Keyboard (CKEY)   Long plastic object often
called into play as weapon during office party recreations of
favorite scenes from American Gladiators. Breaks easily.

Computer Manual (CMA)   Document that comes with a
computer. Written in an alien tongue (*see* Computer) that
only three-year-olds can understand. When translated, tends
to have little relevance to anything the computer does.

Computer Memory (CMO)   What's allegedly inside a
computer.

Computer Programmer (CPROG)   Mad, insane, erratic.
Disordered in mind, passionately preoccupied. Excitable,
capable of being carried away by intense anger.

Computer Screen (CSC)   What's outside a computer.

Cyberspace (CSPCE)   Nineties equivalent of '70s dorm room with Lava Lamp or '80s living room with Ralph Lauren Adirondack furniture, and where everyone sits around acting like boors. The twist is that it doesn't really exist except in the electronic imagination of a computer and its user. Convenient plot device for smarmy sci-fi novels and desperate end-of-season episodes of *Murder, She Wrote.*

Cyberpunk   Someone who knows enough about computers to keep the ones in your office running smoothly, but whom you would prefer not to because of personal hygiene problems or outstanding arrest warrants. *See* Gates, Bill.

E-mail Address   What you want to print on your business cards. Ideally, you want an E-mail address that sounds like a nickname scribbled on a high-school student's notebook. MEATBALL.BRAINS@FINGER.COM and DOUG.THE-SLUG@OUTRAGEOUS.EDU are ideal candidates. E-mail addresses that contain adolescent slang references to body parts and puns on whether or not one is circumcised are especially hot among the Wall Street crowd this year.

Emoticons   Highly sophisticated hieroglyphics used by sophisticated computer users to convey their subtleties of emotion in E-mail messages. All are variants of the infamous "Smiley face." For example: :-) means "I'm smiling!" What most computer users are unaware of is that this cute, seemingly innocuous symbol is interpreted by certain National Security Agency counter-intelligence global E-mail spy scanner computers to mean that the writer has been lobotomized and is flying a hijacked F-14 toward the South Pole to rendezvous with long-suspected-dead members of the Third Reich. It is a good thing that the NSA is so good at cracking computer codes or we would all be doomed.

Evil Geniuses   What I have become convinced most people really, truly in their hearts want to be, as opposed to the kind-hearted dupes that E-mail tends to turn most innocent computer users into.

Flame War   What you can start on Internet by questioning the philosophical depth of *Star Trek* episodes.

Gates, Bill   Evil genius behind software giant Microsoft, who is powerful enough to take over the world—the universe, even. More impressively, he has a shirt that looks like one worn by the head of engineering on the Starship *Enterprise*. (*See* Starship *Enterprise.*) Will be indistinguishable from gray and shrill Ross Perot by year 2010.

Gopher Server   Something on Internet. More importantly, prime example of techno-geek obsession with naming overly complex computer operations after cute rodents.

Harry on CompuServe   An especially disgruntled American voter on CompuServe who thinks that my E-mail address is that of Bill Clinton. "I oppose your crime bill, your health care plan, and all the other socialistic programs you are attempting to dump on the citizens of this nation!" Harry writes me at least once a week. "I feel your pain, Harry," I write back, with a cruel snicker. "Why don't you join me at the Oval Office for lunch and we'll chat about the things that are irritating you." The next week, he writes back, "I oppose any military action in Haiti whatsoever! We have no business there!" "When you get to Washington and want to join me for lunch, Harry," I write back, "ignore the Secret Service agents at the White House gate. Yes, just elbow past them. Shout 'It's me, Harry, from CompuServe!' They'll know what to do." I haven't heard from Harry in a while. I keep watching the news, hoping to find out if he ever made it to his lunch date. That's one of the terrific things about the Information Highway: it gives ordinary people the chance not only to influence the nightly news, but to play with the minds of innocent people.

IBM (IBM)   A computer company that people used to make fun of for being powerful enough to take over the world. (Only in the computer world do people make fun of you because you're powerful enough to take over the world.) Now people make fun of it because it's no longer powerful enough to take over the world.

Idiots (IDT)   Magic word that computer book publishers call their readers in book titles, and which results in obscenely large book sales. What every computer user secretly fears that they are. *See* Dummies.

Information   Something that you have no need to know, that you will never have a need to know, but feel that you must be able to access with your computer in order to keep pace with your business's competitor. *See* Big Information Database.

Information Highway (IH)   Former super-large Department of Defense computer network whose individual components have been obtained by mailing in cereal box tops and dialing local radio call-in contests. Now known as "Internet" and the destination of every American with too much time on her hands. *See* Idiots *and* Waste of Time.

Internet   Large electronic web that puts the world's knowledge at the fingertips of every computer owner, but more importantly allows rumors about planned upcoming *Star Trek* movies to travel quickly to people in impoverished nations.

Internet Football Listserver   The last place I saw my husband. A listserver is a computer on the Internet that stores lists of information, like football statistics, and forwards on messages in a public E-mail discussion. Anyone can access it. The last time I saw my DOH (that's cyberspace slang for "dear old husband") he was huffing and puffing and slugging it out in E-mail with someone who was questioning the fact that the Green Bay Packers continue to be the greatest football team in history. *See* Spousal Abandonment.

Office Computer Guru (OCG)   An extremely intelligent co-worker who is often spotted shuffling disks in and out of computers with a mad passion until administered another dose of electroshock.

Phone Cord (PCD)   Your supposed umbilical cord to the Information Highway. Ninety percent of the sum total of the capital equipment of a frighteningly large number of corporations that have become especially whiny and self-promotional lately. They are also known as "phone companies."

Polynesian Blowfish (PB)   What used to hang in the window of my favorite neighborhood bar.

Spousal Abandonment   What happens when you tell your husband or wife to remind you of their birthday by writing you an E-mail message about it in Internet's talk.bizarre.

Spy Satellite   Spy satellites have nothing to do with this computer book. I wish they did, for certainly this book would be much more interesting if they did.

Starship Enterprise   Next to sex, favorite topic of discussion on former military defense network that has become the Information Highway.

Telecommunications Giant   What everyone claims to be these days.

Vice-President Gore (VPG) Dour elected official who accidentally launched the Information Highway while plugging in a Touch-Tone phone in Oval Office.

Virtual Reality (VR) Similar to cyberspace, but with Lava Lamps. What you experience when you grope around wearing a computerized helmet and sensory gloves, while people giggle at you. Something else in computerdom that doesn't actually exist. Another convenient plot gimmick for smarmy sci-fi novels and end-of-season *Murder, She Wrote* episodes.

Waste of Time What happens when you plug into the Information Highway and start getting lots of E-mail. This book.